# Cambridge Elements ≡

## Elements in Metaphysics
edited by
Tuomas E. Tahko
*University of Bristol*

# METAPHYSICS OF RACE

## Kal H. Kalewold
*University of Leeds*

Shaftesbury Road, Cambridge CB2 8EA, United Kingdom

One Liberty Plaza, 20th Floor, New York, NY 10006, USA

477 Williamstown Road, Port Melbourne, VIC 3207, Australia

314–321, 3rd Floor, Plot 3, Splendor Forum, Jasola District Centre,
New Delhi – 110025, India

103 Penang Road, #05–06/07, Visioncrest Commercial, Singapore 238467

Cambridge University Press is part of Cambridge University Press & Assessment,
a department of the University of Cambridge.

We share the University's mission to contribute to society through the pursuit of
education, learning and research at the highest international levels of excellence.

www.cambridge.org
Information on this title: www.cambridge.org/9781009500302

DOI: 10.1017/9781009241496

First published 2024

*A catalogue record for this publication is available from the British Library*

ISBN 978-1-009-50030-2 Hardback
ISBN 978-1-009-24148-9 Paperback
ISSN 2633-9862 (online)
ISSN 2633-9854 (print)

# Metaphysics of Race

Elements in Metaphysics

DOI: 10.1017/9781009241496
First published online: December 2024

Kal H. Kalewold
*University of Leeds*

**Author for correspondence:** Kal H. Kalewold, k.kalewold@leeds.ac.uk

**Abstract:** Are races real? Is race a biological or social category? What role, if any, does race play in scientific explanations? This Element addresses these and other core questions in the metaphysics of race. It discusses prominent accounts of race such as biological racial realism, social constructivism about race, and racial anti-realism. If anti-realists are right, societies find themselves in thrall to a concept that is scarcely more veridical than "witch" or "werewolf." Social constructionism grounds race in factors ultimately controlled by human thought and action. Biological racial realists argue that race is too quickly dismissed as biologically meaningful, and that it has a role to play in contemporary life sciences. The Element explores these views and shows their virtues and shortcomings. In particular, it advances an argument against biological racial realism that draws on the metaphysics of naturalness and philosophy of biology and medicine.

**Keywords:** race, metaphysics, realism, social constructionism, racial anti-realism

ISBNs: 9781009500302 (HB), 9781009241489 (PB), 9781009241496 (OC)
ISSNs: 2633-9862 (online), 2633-9854 (print)

# Contents

## 1 Introduction

*Race* names the primary subdivision of the human species. What kind of division that is – whether essential, biological, social, or otherwise – has historically been one of the most contested questions in the study of human diversity. There is also debate about whether the thing race name exists at all. The concept of race has been intertwined with and profoundly consequential for the sociopolitical and economic history of the last several centuries. Race (or racialism) is indispensable to understanding historical developments including the discovery and conquest of the Americas (by Europeans), the transatlantic slave trade, the plantation systems of the New World, the colonization of Africa, the emergence of nationalism in Europe, decolonization, among many others. Nor can race be properly understood without the contexts in which many of the ideas associated with the concept of race became salient. This makes the metaphysics of race an ecumenical area of study informed by, among other things, philosophy, biology, linguistics, history, and economics.

This Cambridge Element proceeds first by briefly tracing the historical development of the race concept and many of the properties associated with race (1.1). Section 1.2 discusses race essentialism and how its defining conditions shaped the ordinary concept of race. In Section 2, I trace contemporary biology of human diversity. Unsurprisingly, modern research in evolutionary biology, genetics, and anthropology has discredited essentialist conceptions of human races. However, biological racial realists argue that race can be rescued from essentialist premises and grounded in modern scientific research programs. Section 2.1 discusses varieties of biological racial realism. In particular, I focus on what I consider to be the most promising attempt to ground the biological genuineness of race, namely, accounts of minimalist biological race defended by Michael O. Hardimon and Quayshawn Spencer.

However, I argue that these (minimalist) biological races fail to count as genuine biological kinds or entities. The thing that made race essentialism false is also, perhaps ironically, what makes essentialist races good candidates for genuine kinds or entities. That is, essential conceptions of race identify race as robustly explanatory of a range of regularities including behavior, psychological capacities, and even aesthetic preferences. Of course, it is false that race is explanatorily connected to these regularities. The minimalist and deflationary approach that biological racial realists take rightly eschews this essentialist thesis. Nonetheless, this has the effect of rendering the resulting putative kinds or entities inapt. In Section 2.7, I advance a Gerrymandering Objection to minimalist biological races. I argue that minimalist biological races are gerrymandered kinds or entities. They lack the dimensions of explanatory value that natural or genuine biological kinds or entities possess. As a result, they are not apt to play a role in scientific explanation, causation, prediction, and so on.

Race, of course, is not only to be understood as part of the natural order of things. An influential metaphysical approach conceives of race as a mainly or solely social (or cultural) phenomenon. Race, on this broad approach, is the result of human thought and action. The most prominent way to cash this out is the view that race is socially constructed. Social construction about race (or racial constructionism) is open to a number of divergent, and sometimes contradictory, interpretations. Section 3 discusses political and cultural constructionism about race, as well as prominent accounts of each. I also discuss topics in the social metaphysics of race including the relationship between social constructionism and biological racial realism (3.5) and race and social structural explanation (Section 3.6).

The Element closes with a discussion of anti-realism about race (Section 4). This isn't to say that anti-realism is an inevitable conclusion of philosophical reflection on race. Rather, understanding the motivation for anti-realism benefits from the discussion of the previous sections, from the rise and fall of race essentialism to the philosophical challenges faced by accounts of biological or social realism about race. Anti-realists draw on the contingency of race concepts in many societies, the (false) essentialist origins of many aspects of the ordinary concept of race, and the analogy of race with discarded, but historically widespread, concepts about human kinds to contest the meaningfulness of race. The section discusses the most prominent tool in the philosophical arsenal of racial anti-realism: the mismatch objection (Section 4.1). Anti-realists argue that race is an illusion, yet not any less consequential for it.

## 1.1 What Is Race?

A natural launching point for an exploration of whether race *exists* is to ask what race *is*. That is, what are we talking about when we talk about race? As is standard in philosophy, we can begin by probing what we ordinarily mean by race, that is, how race is used in our everyday discourse. The *ordinary concept of race* is meant to capture what we commonly mean when we use the word "race" and its cognates. Consider the following statements:

> "Barack Obama was elected the first black president in American history";
> "While black Americans live four years fewer than whites, black Britons live longer than their white compatriots[1]"

---

[1] Taken from the following report by Burn-Murdoch (2023): www.ft.com/content/a2050877-124a-472d-925a-fc794737d814

"Amid ongoing reports of racially motivated threats and attacks against Asians in the United States, a majority of Asian Americans say violence against them is increasing[2] ... "

These statements involve what we might call *race talk*. They refer to categories – black, white, Asian – that we, competent (English) language users engaging in our everyday mainstream discursive practices, take to be racial. The ordinary concept of race captures much of what this mainstream race talk is pointing toward. There are two desiderata for an analysis of the ordinary concept of race. It needs to capture much of the common sense or traditional racial beliefs that prevail in most societies. And it needs to be compatible with a wide range of theories of race, from essentialism to anti-realism. That is, the ordinary concept of race is defined such that various metaphysical positions in the debate are prima facie talking about the same thing.[3] Hardimon's (2003) account of the ordinary concept of race fulfills both these desiderata.[4] Of course, as we will see in the coming sections, whether or not the race concept necessarily entails substantive metaphysical commitments is open to debate.

Hardimon (2003) identifies the "logical core" of the ordinary concept of race to consist of three premises. First, Races are *groups* of human beings. These groups of humans are distinguishable from other groups of humans by "visible physical features of the relevant kind" (Hardimon 2003, 442). The relevant visible physical features that distinguish between races are (at least superficially) biological. They should be salient and easily identifiable by the naked eye. The most common candidates for these distinguishing features are skin color, eye shape, nose shape, and lip form, among others. These traits are *phenotypes*, which are the expressed or manifested result of (as we now know) genetic and developmental mechanisms. Racial groups need not differ from one another in all these features, nor will all members of a racial group have all and only those features associated with their race.

Second, members of a racial group are linked by common ancestry. Different theories of race will vary in how they draw the connection between race and ancestry. Nonetheless, the ordinary concept of race is "something inherited, a property transmitted from generation to generation" (Hardimon 2003, 446). If two individuals of the same race, *R*, have biological offspring, that offspring is

---

[2] Pew Research Center (2022): www.pewresearch.org/short-reads/2022/05/09/about-a-third-of-asian-americans-say-they-have-changed-their-daily-routine-due-to-concerns-over-threats-attacks/

[3] As Hardimon (2003, 450) puts it, "it is because essentialist and anti-essentialist conceptions of race share a common subject matter fixed by the ordinary concept or race that they are able to contradict one another."

[4] Throughout this Element reference to the *ordinary concept of race* appeals to the characterization defended by Hardimon (2003).

also a member of $R$ by virtue of his or her ancestry. This lineage can be traced back to a founder group. What makes a lineage racial is that the founder groups are distinguishable from one another by visible physical features which are in turn retained by their descendants. As such, two groups whose members have the same visible physical features but do not descend from the same common founder group are not of the same race.

The third, and final, thesis is that each race is associated with a geographic location. Intuitively, racial groups have distinct geographic origins. Continents, given their size and relative isolation, play the role of specific geographic locations associated with each race: black from (Sub-Saharan) Africa, white from Europe, Asians from (East) Asia, and so on. This fact grounds an important feature of the ordinary concept of race, namely, that races were geographically isolated from one another before the emergence of sophisticated forms of transport. This separation led to reproductive isolation and precipitated the emergence of the racial traits that differentiate racial groups. Hardimon notes we can interpret the visible physical traits that differentiate races as adaptations to local geographic conditions (Hardimon 2003, 448). However, pre-Darwinian theories of race posited their own explanations of the cause of racial traits (see Section 1.1).

The ordinary concept of race is compatible with a wide range of different *conceptions* of race. Following Hardimon (2003) and Glasgow (2009), I draw a distinction throughout this Element between *a concept* of race and a *conception* of race. As Hardimon (2003, 439) writes,

> It is part of the idea of a concept that one and the same concept can be articulated in a number of different and competing ways. It is part of the idea of a conception that a conception represents but one of a number of possible different and competing ways in which a given concept can be articulated.

Glasgow (2009) likens the concept/conception distinction to one between meanings and theories (Glasgow 2009, 23). A concept picks out the *subject* of one's discussion whereas a conception is a fleshed-out theory about that subject. For instance, it belongs to the concept of humans, among other things, that humans are mammals. If someone were to point to some X and (literally) claim "this reptile is a human," they have made an error as to the subject of their speech. Whereas a conception of humans can hold that humans were directly created by God and have an immortal soul; an alternative conception may hold humans are part of an evolutionary lineage stretching back millions of years. These are two rival *conceptions* of the same *concept*. They are talking about the same subject but have different theories as to that subject. That is, if two people disagree on their *concepts*, they are talking about different things. If they disagree on their *conceptions* of the same concept, they are disagreeing about what features or properties the concept has.

Armed with the concept/conception distinction, we can see the ordinary concept should be conceived of as *thin*. It does not, for instance, commit to the view that races have *essences* (i.e., that races have "fixed and immutable" properties) or that race membership is biologically significant across many dimensions. The ordinary concept of race is also silent on whether there is a racial hierarchy and whether moral and intellectual capacities vary by race. The ordinary race concept does, however, purport to refer to something *biological*. The visible physical features that distinguish races are the product of biological processes. Furthermore, both ancestry and geography are directly or indirectly taken to play a biologically significant role in, at the least, the emergence and perpetuation of (racial) visible morphological traits such as skin color.

However, as Glasgow (2009) notes, philosophers of race have proposed other, thicker, accounts of the (ordinary) concept of race. Thicker accounts of the concept of race add conditions to the "logical core" that go beyond what Hardimon (2003) identifies. For instance, holding that the concept of race entails the racial purity of the majority of humans (Zack 1993); that race is ordinarily understood as both biological and sociopolitical (Outlaw 1996); or that races are ordinarily taken to have biobehavioral essences (Hirschfeld 1996), among others. Whether or not these views are correct requires detailed philosophical analysis and experimental evidence drawing on the social science of perceptions of race (Glasgow 2009). Nonetheless, I will rely on Hardimon's (2003) thin conception in subsequent sections because it is fairly intuitive and allows us to examine the widest range of conceptions of race.

To begin (near) the beginning of modern race theorizing, let us first consider the essentialist conception of race.

## 1.2 Race Essentialism

Race essentialism[5] is a conception of race that holds that race is a natural, fixed, and immutable division of humans into discreet groups. On the essentialist view, race divides humans into biobehaviorally distinct groups. The differences between races are responsible for the social, cultural, and intellectual disparities among racial groups. Consequently, race essentialism often assumes a racial hierarchy. Essentialism is a discredited theory of race with virtually no proponents within the wider scientific and philosophical community working on issues

---

[5] Some authors use the term *racialism or racialist race* to refer to this view. See Shelby (2005, 209) and Hardimon (2017a).

intersecting with race. Nonetheless, an exploration of race essentialism is useful on two counts. First, many ordinary racial ideas were developed at the same time that essentialism about race was dominant (Appiah 1996; Hardimon 2003). Understanding many of the suppositions that come with race talk is not possible except in the context of the emergence of the race concept and race essentialism in the eighteenth century (whether or not it may be possible to liberate it from that context). Second, race essentialism, although false, possesses many features of a conceptual analysis for a genuine kind that sheds light on the shortcomings of latter realist, but nonessentialist, views of race. That is, race essentialism conceives of race as an explanatorily rich category, one that is robustly connected to explaining cultural, psychological, physiological, and other phenomena (see Section 2.6).

An essentialist[6] conception of race has three defining conditions[7]:

(1)  Humans can be subdivided into (ordinary) races.
(2)  Individuals from different (ordinary) races are more different from one another than individuals of the same (ordinary) race.
(3)  Differences between the (ordinary) races explain differences in behavior, culture, psychological traits, and health and vigor.

Race essentialism, at least in its modern form, traces to the emerging taxonomic practices of the eighteenth century. Carl Linnaeus (1707–1778), in his groundbreaking *Systema Naturae* (1735), provided one of the first systematic taxonomies of human variation. The Linnaean system classified humans into four variants: *Europaeus albescens, Americanus rubescens, Asiaticus fuscus,* and *Africanus nigriculus.* Linnaeus took these to be varieties of humans ("homo variat"). The association between human variation and skin color implied by his naming convention – yellowish Asians, blackish Africans, and so on – remained a prominent element of subsequent racial classification. The early editions of the *Systema,* a work he continually revised, only included skin color and geography as the relevant differences between races. Furthermore, races were not conceived as subspecies, a type of subclassification Linnaeus deployed in the case of plants and animals, but rather as *variants* of humans.

The tenth edition of the *Systema* expanded the section on the human *genus*. In this edition, however, races were identified not only with skin color and geography but also with other physical, moral, and cultural attributes. The four races, corresponding to four continents, were also associated with the

---

[6]  See also Appiah (1996), 54.
[7]  There are of course other ways of characterizing race essentialism (cf. Mallon 2016, 18). My account has two virtues: it captures a wide range of theories commonly taken to be essentialist while at the same time being distinct from biological racial realism.

four humors (phlegm, blood, black bile, and yellow bile) whose specific proportions in the body were taken to explain temperament and disease. To skin color, other physical features such as hair texture, eye shape, and lip form were added. Additionally, Linnaeus attributed traits ranging from aesthetic judgment to preference for forms of government to racial differences (Müller-Wille 2014).

For instance, *Homo sapiens* europaeus is white, sanguine, has straight, yellow hair, is inventive, and governed by rites. *Homo sapiens* americanus is red, choleric, has thick black hair, cheerful of disposition, and is governed by customary right. And so on for each race. With the tenth edition, then, we see much more explanatory significance given to race. Not only is race merely a matter of geography and some climate-related traits, but it is also connected to a host of factors including behavior, health, and mental and cultural capacities and practices. This characterization of race and human variation deeply influenced subsequent developments in anthropology and human biology (Marks 2007).

Kenan Malik (1996) and Justin E. H. Smith (2015) crucially highlight the fact that the history of the development of racial theory is not uniform. The contestation of eighteenth-century Enlightenment values played a role in shaping early race theorizing. For some, common humanity, the universality of reason, and belief in progress found expression in their race theorizing in defenses of monogenism[8] and a limited conception of racial difference that attributed variation between races to differences in climate, diet, and lifestyle. No figure better represents the tension between the Enlightenment commitments to universal humanity and the essentialist theorizing of race of the nineteenth and twentieth centuries than Johann Blumenbach.

Johann Friedrich Blumenbach (1752–1840), a leading figure in the development of anthropology, proposed perhaps the most influential racial classification system. Blumenbach's classification had two major differences from Linnaeus'. First, Blumenbach argued skull shape and size are the defining characteristics of races. Second, Blumenbach's classification scheme identified five, rather than four, races: Caucasian, Mongolian, Ethiopian, American, and Malay. Both the five-race schema and the use of race categories such as "Caucasian" were widely adopted in subsequent racial theories (Malik 1996). Although skeletal craniotomy became a favored tool in the arsenal of essentialist race realism, Blumenbach rejected both polygenism and racial theories that posit deep racial differences (Smith 2015). For Blumenbach, racial boundaries are arbitrary and

---

[8] *Polygenism* is a theory of human origins that holds that the human species had multiple distinct origins. *Monogenism*, by contrast, holds that the human species has a single origin.

"whatever we might ascribe to racial difference can be accounted for almost exclusively in terms of climate, and color in particular is so superficial that it can easily change over the course of an individual's life, either through changes in diet or climate, or simply through internal changes in the life cycle, of the same sort as we see in the graying of hair" (Smith 2015, 256). For Blumenbach, race is ultimately inconsequential when considered against the naturally more determinative division between species.

Blumenbach's work represents a path untraveled in the development of racial science. His limited approach was eclipsed by the far more dominant essentialist theories of race. In the history of western philosophy, no less prominent figures than David Hume and Immanuel Kant were proponents of race essentialism. Hume rejected monogenism and embraced a polygenic and hierarchical race theory (Malik 1996, 53). Hume held racial differences to be substantial and to be caused by not only physical but also moral factors such as culture, custom, and psychology (Zack 2018, 12 f). Furthermore, races are hierarchically placed in relation to several capacities including intelligence.

Immanuel Kant's writings on human diversity are broadly representative of the emerging essentialist conception that dominated nineteenth-century race theory. Kant outlined in his anthropology a view of race that combined the defining conditions of race essentialism. Unlike Hume, Kant was a monogenist. Nevertheless, Kant took race to be an intermediate category between species and variation (Kleingeld 2007, 578). In his 1775 essay *On the Different Races of Man*, Kant defines races as "those which, when transplanted (displaced to other areas), maintain themselves over protracted generations, and which also generate hybrid young whenever they interbreed with other deviations of the same stock[9]" (Kant 1775, 39). The "deviations" that are definitional of races are heritable. They perpetuate even if members of a race migrate away from their geographic regions. And "inter-breeding" between "deviations" produces "half-breeds" with mixed characteristics. The difference between individuals of the same race, on the other hand, is merely variation.[10]

In an illustrative passage, Kant writes:

> Negroes and whites are not different species of human beings (since they presumably belong to one stock), but they are different races, for each perpetuates itself in every area, and they generate between them children

---

[9] All Kant quotes are from translations published in *Race and the Enlightenment: A Reader*, edited by Emmanuel Chukwudi Eze (Oxford: Wiley-Blackwell, 1997).

[10] Kant's reasoning about the varieties of human variation is puzzling. The fact that the skin color of "mixed race" children is liable to "blending" whereas the hair color of monoracial children does not blend the (different) hair color of their parents hardly illuminates the structure of human variation. While Kant cannot be faulted for not knowing genetics, many other examples he could have chosen (such as height) cut against the deviation/variation line he draws.

that are necessarily hybrid, or blendings (mulattoes). On the other hand, blonds or brunettes are not different races of whites, for a blond man can also ger from a brunette woman altogether blond children … (40)

Kant's views in this passage capture condition (ii) of essentialist races. Although there is *variation* between individuals of the same race, these are not significant. For instance, some white people have blue while others have brown eyes. Notable *deviations* occur between individuals of different races. This interracial difference is so great that interbreeding between races produces "half-breed" children, while interbreeding between variants of the same race does not require such designation.

Furthermore, Kant's race theory is hierarchical[11] and holds that differences in nonphysical properties such as intelligence, culture, temperament, and so on are a consequence of racial differences. In a hallmark of race essentialist accounts, Kant draws an explanatory relation between climate, geography, physical features, and psychological and behavioral traits. Of the "negro" race, for instance, Kant writes " … the Negro is … well suited to his climate; that is, strong, fleshy, supple, but in the midst of the bountiful provision of his motherland lazy, soft and dawdling" (46). The tension between commitment to both the contingency of the origins of (racial) physical human diversity and the absence of even the possibility of intellectual achievement among those Kant considers racially inferior is a curious aspect of Kant's thought. It suggests at the very least that racism played a significant role in Kant's racial theorizing (Smith 2015, 235).

The racial theories of Kant and Hume did not go unchallenged by contemporaries. Johann Gottfried von Herder (1744–1803) rejected Kant's racialized and hierarchical understanding of human difference. As mentioned above, many enlightenment figures emphasized common humanity and the ability of all humans to reason. Herder, a leading figure of the Romantic reaction to the Enlightenment, emphasized culturalist and national differences to defend the dignity of different "races." For Herder, reason is embodied in and manifests through culture. And all human cultures manifest reason in their particular way. As such, there is no independent (which is to say, Eurocentric) ground from which to dismiss the capacities and way of life of nonwhite people (Smith 2015, 231–233). However, later adopters of the Herder's approach integrated it

---

[11] Kleingeld (2007) argues that Kant changed his mind on the hierarchical view of races he developed in the 1790s. I do not here take a view as to whether racial hierarchy was an element of Kant's final, mature thought. Whether or not it was subsequently revised, Kant's race theory illuminates what became the dominant conception of race in the 19th century. See also Huaping Lu-Adler (2023) for a book-length treatment of the relationship between Kant's raceology and his wider philosophical work.

seamlessly with the dominant racial and racist thought of the nineteenth century. As Malik (1996) notes, "once it was accepted that different peoples were motivated by particular sentiments, unique to themselves, it was but a short step to view these differences as racial" (Malik 1996, 79).

The nineteenth century was the era of what became known as "scientific racism." Race theories from this period moved further away from some of the shared assumptions of enlightenment figures writing about race and human differences. The belief in common humanity was de-emphasized or outright rejected. Hierarchy became a defining element of racial classification extending beyond what many eighteenth-century theorists proposed (Malik 1996). Polygenism gained wider acceptance. Race theory and racism became inextricably linked. The fact that the nineteenth century saw the most intense period of European colonialism and the exploitation of black slave labor in the United States, the Caribbean, and Latin America played a large role in determining which race theories found wide purchase (Smith 2015, 229 f). As Zack (2018) argues, racial theories that dominated Western societies in this period served to uphold the social order and licensing practices such as slavery and white supremacy (see Section 3).

Race essentialism had its heyday in the period between the early nineteenth century and the Second World War. The race essentialist underpinnings of Nazi ideology were a death knell for the view in the postwar period. In an influential Statement on Race issued by the newly formed UNESCO in 1950, a distinguished panel of biologists and social scientists were charged with addressing race and racism in light of the events leading up to the Second World War and its aftermath (UNESCO 1950). The Statement recognized that humans can be biologically subdivided into smaller groups, and these groups can be considered races. Nonetheless, the Statement rejected the claim that temperament, personality, character, and other innate mental characteristics were racial traits. Furthermore, developments in human biology and genetics made some claims that were associated with or integral to race essentialism, such as polygenism or racialized psychology, untenable (see Section 2). Nonetheless, a complex set of questions about the relationship between race, biology, and genetics still remained to be answered. In the next section, I discuss contemporary scientific work on human diversity and discuss a range of views defending the biological genuineness of race, namely, biological racial realism.

## 2 Race and the Biology of Human Difference

In a reported essay for *Harper's Magazine*, Kritika Varagur documents a tragic aspect of contemporary Nigerian society. Varagur follows Nigerian couples navigating romance in the face of a troubling genetic fact, nearly a quarter of Nigeria's population are "silent" carriers of an abnormal copy of the hemoglobin gene. Six million Nigerians have both abnormal copies and consequently suffer from sickle cell disease (SCD), a blood disorder causing complications including blood clots and pain (see Section 2.10). Any children of carriers and sufferers from SCD have a 50 percent chance of developing SCD. In the age of genetic testing, potential Nigerian couples are confronted with the possibility that those they fall in love with, and with whom they plan to start a family, may pass on a debilitating genetic disease to their children.

As we shall see in Section 2.9, sickle cell disease is among a handful of genetic disorders where race is proposed to play a prominent role in its research, diagnosis, and treatment. The genetic variant responsible for SCD is not randomly distributed across human populations. In order to see how this fact is defended by some biological racial realists as demonstrating the explanatory potential of a biological conception of race, let us first briefly trace contemporary biological understanding of human origins and human diversity.

There are three main interrelated research areas that inform our understanding of race and whether and in what form it may be considered biological. These are (1) the evolutionary history of the human species (including its origins and patterns of dispersion and settlement), (2) population genetics, and (3) the study and treatment of genetic diseases. As to the area (1), the most prominent current theory of human origins holds that modern humans originated in Africa some 150–200 thousand years ago. Populations of humans began to disperse throughout the rest of the world in an east-to-west pattern beginning in Eurasia and ending in the Americas. In the process of human dispersal out of Africa, populations encountered other hominid species such as Neanderthals and Denisovans, and (occasionally) interbred. The bottleneck effect of a smaller population migrating out of Africa and subsequent splinter subpopulations migrating farther afield explains why genetic diversity within populations decreases as the geographic distance from Africa increases. It also accounts for why of the relatively few alleles that are unique to individual regions, half are found in Africa (Rosenberg 2011).

This broad account is of course too simple. Populations do not only migrate away but also migrate back. For instance, a study by Chen and colleagues (2020) has found Neanderthal ancestry in Africans. This is likely due to gene flow between Eurasian *Homo sapiens* (who interbred with Neanderthals) and African *Homo sapiens* populations resulting from migration back from Eurasia to Africa (Chen et al. 2020). Continental "barriers" do not in each instance impose discrete segmentation of human populations. Rather, some continental human populations (e.g., Eurasia and Africa) are *clinal*, rather than discrete.

That is, they are characterized by gradual variation of character across a range (e.g., clinal gradation in skin color). Even if, say, Polynesia and Africa are separated with historically insurmountable geographic barriers, the parent populations of both groups could have had gene flow far more recently than the migration patterns would suggest. In any case, most genetics and archeological findings support the broad Out of Africa narrative.

The twenty-first century has seen immense progress in the investigation of the genetic structure of human populations. The completion of the Human Genome Project in stages between 1990 and 2021, which produced sequence data for the entire human genome, made an immense contribution to the study of human genetic diversity. Rosenberg and colleagues' (2002) landmark study used a model-based clustering algorithm called *structure* to identify major "genetic clusters" based on the distribution of multifocal alleles. Their approach did not rely on information about the sampling location of individuals. Instead of measuring the genetic distance between samples from pre-defined groups, *structure* was used to generate population clusters of genetic similarity from HGDP-CEPH human genome diversity cell line panel, which was drawn from individuals from fifty-two populations around the world. The algorithm was used to generate $K$ number of clusters (with $K$ chosen in advance) with distinctive allele frequencies. At $K = 2$, *structure* identified two groups, one centered in Africa and the other in America, consistent with the genetic distance between these two cluster centers.

A remarkable finding is that, at $K = 5$, *structure* identified clusters corresponding to the five major continental regions: Africa, Eurasia, East Asia, America, and Oceania.[12]

Rosenberg and colleagues (2002) report a number of findings, supported by subsequent research (see Rosenberg et al. 2005, Rosenberg 2011), that have implications for the viability of a biogenetic race concept. First, nearly 95 per cent of genetic differences are between individuals. Genetic differences between individuals from different clusters are only slightly greater than unrelated individuals within a cluster. Second, region-specific alleles are rare on two counts: (i) most alleles are found in either every region or in more than one region, and (ii) alleles found in only one region are rare within that region. As they note "this overall similarity of human populations is also evident in the

---

[12] Rosenberg and colleagues (2002) do not identify these clusters as races. However, their findings, as well as other similar clustering-based studies of human genetic structure, is taken by (minimal) biological racial realists as evidence for their view. After all, these five geographic genetic clusters correspond to minimalist races, a la Hardimon (2017a,b) and to the OMB racial classification widely used in the United States as discussed by Spencer (2018) and Glasgow et al. (2019). See Section 2.5.

geographically widespread nature of most alleles ... region-specific alleles were usually rare, with a median relative frequency of 1.0% in their region of occurrence" (Rosenberg et al. 2002, 2381–2382). In other words, there are no locally common region-specific alleles (Long, Li, and Healy 2009). Third, many individuals can be assigned to more than one cluster, reflecting the clinal nature of genetic differences.

The fact that there are no genetic variants that all and only (or even many) members of one geographic region possess, that many individuals can be assigned to more than one cluster, and that genetic variation between clusters is a relatively small amount of overall genetic variation has important upshots for a theory of race. For one, it makes race essentialism impossible to defend on genetic grounds. Indeed, race essentialism is a holdover from pre-Darwinian understanding of species and types (Pigliucci and Kaplan 2003). The fact that genetic variation in humans is mostly between individuals and that between-group variation is greatest within local population groups, has been so frequently cited against race essentialism as to be the chief instrument of its death (Lewontin 1972; Gould 1996).[13]

However, a view that holds that races are biological need not be *essentialist*. Biological racial realists defend accounts of biological race that reject essentialist assumptions, one of which (the second condition of race essentialism Section 1.2) is the idea that races vary along multiple behavioral and cognitive traits.

## 2.1 Varieties of Biological Racial Realism

*Biological racial realism*[14] holds that races are biologically meaningful categories that capture or correspond to at least one structure of human diversity. There are many ways that race can be biological – genetic, cladistic, ecotypical – depending on what factors are taken to be the biological basis of race. Nonetheless, biological racial realists take the biological basis of race to be more than the physical features (e.g., skin color) that are ordinarily taken to be racial.

---

[13] It is important to note that for Lewontin (1972) the claim is not just that any biological grouping of humans fails to capture our folk or ordinary concept of race. Rather, he argues there is no biological grouping of humans that captures the *social significance* that race has. As Lewontin put it in the conclusion of his groundbreaking paper challenging a biogenetic race concept, "it is clear that our perception of relatively large differences between human races and subgroups, as compared to variations within these groups, is indeed a biased perception [...]" and therefore "human racial classification is of no social value and is positively destructive of social and human relations. Since such racial classification is seen to be of no genetic or taxonomic significance either, no justification can be offered for its continuance" (Lewontin 1972, 397).

[14] This view is sometimes called *racial naturalism* (see Mallon 2006; Hochman 2013; Spencer 2014).

Next, let us examine proposals by Robin Andreasen and Phillip Kitcher to defend the biological reality of race on the grounds that races are *isolated breeding populations*.

## 2.2 Races as Breeding Populations

Andreasen (1998, 2000, 2004) defends a cladistic theory of race. The cladistic race concept defines races by means of a single property: shared genealogy. Cladistics is a system of classification that categorizes taxa solely based on genealogy. As such, according to the cladistic race concept, races are clades. One race is distinct from another not in virtue of genetic variation or differences in visible biophysical features (although they may vary along these dimensions). Rather, races are classified on the basis of their distinct genealogies. Andreasen defends a view where "races are ancestor-descendant sequences of breeding populations that share a common origin" (Andreasen 2004, 425), where *breeding populations* are "a set of local populations that are reproductively connected to one another and [are] reasonably reproductively isolated from other such sets" (426). Races become distinct when populations branch out and, for whatever reason, become reproductively isolated. This reproductive isolation leads to genetic distance as the separate populations undergo distinct evolutionary pathways (Andreasen 1998, 2000, 2004).

Andreasen constructs a human phylogenetic tree to represent the branching (and isolation) of human breeding populations that form the cladistic races. Consistent with the Out of Africa thesis, the trunk of the tree represents modern humans in Africa some 200 thousand years ago. The tips of the trees are current breeding populations (i.e., cladistic races), with each branching point representing the formation of a new breeding population. On this basis, Andreasen identifies nine cladistic races: New Guinea and Australia, Pacific Islander, Southeast Asian, Northeast Asian, Arctic Northeast Asian, Amerindian, European, Non-European Caucasoid (Andreasen 2004, 458).

It is important to note that cladistic races are *dynamic*. That is, it is possible that after mass migration and the breakdown of isolating factors, cladistic races come to cease to exist. If two initially isolated breeding populations begin to interbreed, then they no longer constitute different cladistic races. It is also possible that new forms of isolation emerge that generate branching forming novel cladistic races. Suppose for instance that humans establish a suitably large colony on Mars but, for some reason, this colony is cut off from Earth. If there are no barriers to interbreeding within the Martian colony, "Martian" would constitute a new cladistic race of the human species.

Andreasen argues that there are several virtues of the cladistic account. First, cladistics provides a biological conception of race. After all, evolutionary biology is centrally concerned with reproductive relations, genealogy, and genetic distance. A cladistic account defines race with the same conceptual tools used to define speciation, a core explanatory target of evolutionary biology. Second, cladistic race also avoids two major challenges to a biological conception of race: the genetic and independent variation arguments.

The "genetic argument" against biological race holds that since common-sense racial categories do not track significant patterns of human genetic diversity, they are not biologically meaningful. As discussed in Section 2, Variation among individuals within the same population represents the over-whelming majority of human genetic diversity. Of the remaining fraction of human genetic diversity, variation between individuals of different (racial) genetic clusters is only slightly greater than variation between unrelated individuals within (racial) genetic clusters.[15] As such, race is not meaningfully biological. Andreasen (2004) argues cladistic race concept sidesteps the genetic argument since it does not conceive of race as a *genetic* category. Races are defined *solely* through genealogy, regardless of what share of genetic diversity (if any) is between breeding populations constituting cladistic races.

The "independent variation argument" denies the biological reality of races by targeting the lack of coherence between racial categories and their defining racial traits. That is, traits such as skin color vary independently from traits such as hair texture, and so on. While one or two traits may provide an unambiguous racial classification scheme, the more traits are used the more cross-variance occurs. Consequently, proponents of the independent variation argument maintain that "because there is no non-arbitrary way to choose one classification scheme over another, we ought to abandon biological racial classification altogether" (Andreasen 2004, 428). Once again, the cladistic race concept is able to avoid this challenge. Biophysical traits play no role in the delineation of cladistic races. As a result, cladistic races do not correspond to the ordinary, or "folk," racial groups such as "black, Asian, and white." The aim of the cladistic account is not to license the biological reality of existing racial categories. Rather, it is meant to rescue race as a biological category by severing it from the often incoherent and biased forms of folk racial classification.

---

[15] Andreasen (2004) cites different results from the ones I use (i.e., Rosenberg et al. 2002) to outline the genetic argument. The specific figures in (Andreasen 2004, 428) are drawn from older research into apportionment of human genetic diversity explicitly comparing inter and intra-racial group protein and DNA polymorphisms. However, this change does not alter the thrust of the genetic argument.

However, the supposed virtues of the cladistic account in blocking challenges to the biological reality of race bring into question whether cladistic race is a conception or theory of *race* at all.[16] As Hardimon (2003) argues, the logical core of the ordinary race concept, even the relatively thin account he defends, involves more than mere genealogy. Andreasen (2004) contends the divergence between cladistic and "common sense" racial categories is not a problem for the cladistic view. After all, as Andreasen (2004) notes, "there has always been widespread disagreement over how many racial categories there are and who belongs to what category" (Andreasen 2004, 437). The existence of multiple incompatible racial classification schemes does not invalidate the fact that any given conception is a conception of *race*.

Nevertheless, the divergence between the cladistic and ordinary race concepts remains objectionable because the cladistic concept fails to match *any* of the dominant conceptions of race (Glasgow 2003, 460). While common ancestry is an intuitively central aspect of the race concept, physical resemblance also plays a central role. If, As Andreasen contends, it is possible for different cladistic breeding populations to be physically indistinguishable from one another, it is hard to see how they can be different *races*. It seems then that Andreasen is not vindicating the biological reality of races but defending an alternative approach to apportioning humans into smaller groups.

Furthermore, Spencer (2012) argues that the cladistic race concept has not been shown to provide explanatory or predictive power in cladistics (Spencer 2012, 203). The cladistic race concept has not caught on in the research programs investigating human diversity and population structure and the nine cladistic races have found little purchase within the scientific or broader community. There is a good reason why genetics is a flashpoint of debates around the biological viability of race. And that is because genetic diversity captures a lot of what we care about in broader debates about the usefulness of race as a biological category in, for instance, medicine and psychology. The cladistic account does not connect race to these areas of central concern.

Kitcher (1999, 2007) defends a biological conception of race that draws on his broader pragmatic approach to science.[17] Kitcher argues that it is possible to defend an account of race as a biological subdivision of humans. However, this racial delineation is not a purely biological matter. Crucially, whether a biological conception of race ought to be deployed will partially depend on whether it serves a value we (well-informed, deliberatively democratic agents) endorse in a way that exceeds the costs of racialization.

---

[16] This is the Mismatch Objection discussed in 4.1. See also Section 1.1.

[17] See Kitcher (2001) for a full view of Kitcher's seminal account of science and its relationship to democracy.

Kitcher defends a biological account of race that he argues answers to these requirements. On Kitcher's account, as in Andreasen's, races are *isolated breeding populations*. Kitcher grounds his analysis in ordinary biological practice. As noted by Andreasen, evolutionary biologists are centrally concerned with speciation. Kitcher argues an obvious way to begin conceptualizing biological race is to first approach biological species concepts. The dominant biological account of species holds that species are clusters of populations that (1) would freely interbreed in the wild and (2) are separated from other interbreeding clusters by reproductive isolation (Kitcher 2007, 295). Reproductive isolation is sometimes the result of geographic isolation, but it need not be. Co-located clusters can be reproductively isolated by behavioral, morphological, or temporal factors (e.g., nocturnal vs. diurnal cycles).

Additionally, as part of this general account of species, it is possible to divide species into local varieties or "races." These *subspecies* are the result of *reduced* interbreeding. That is, within a subspecies "it is considerably more probable that members of the population will mate with one another than with outsiders" (296). Subspecies are often distinguishable from one another by differences in phenotypic traits that arose as a result of generations of isolated inbreeding. These subspecies are races. A race on Kitcher's account is "an inbred lineage, where the inbreeding may initially have resulted from geographical isolation that eventually gives rise to differences in phenotype and to some interference in free interbreeding, even when the geographical isolation is overcome" (Kitcher 2007, 296).

Kitcher's account differs from Andreasen's on two points. First, on Kitcher's conception phenotypic or genetic distinctness does play a role in racial classification. Second, races can be maintained even in the aftermath of human mass migration between different geographic regions. Kitcher argues this is due to the fact that social factors now play the role of isolating mechanisms once played by geographic separation. In the United States, social and cultural factors sustain racial inbreeding and prevent racial coupling and intermarriage (Kitcher 1999, 98). What maintains races in this context is that "these people belong to a different race because they were once *labeled* – mistakenly, ignorantly, unreasonably – as intrinsically different, for that initial labeling has given rise to the separation of their way of life from that of the labelers" (Kitcher 2007, 298). As such, race is both socially constructed and biologically real. And it is the social construction that keeps race biologically real.

Kitcher's defense of the biological reality of race is open to the same criticism as Andreasen's. Namely, it is not clear that the groupings identified by Kitcher's account are *races* as ordinarily understood (Glasgow 2003). Kitcher's account goes beyond trimming and adjustment that concepts may undergo as part of a rigorous analysis. For one, the number of populations that have reduced levels of interbreeding far exceeds the number of races proposed by any dominant conception of race. Observable differences in the distribution of allele frequencies occur between dozens of populations that have reduced interbreeding due to, for instance, linguistic barriers[18] (Hellwege et al. 2017). Additionally, as Glasgow (2003) notes, in so far as the conception of race Kitcher defends rests on reproductive isolation, different social classes with social barriers to inbreeding may qualify as races (Glasgow 2003, 470). Once again, there is a divergence between the conception proposed and the concept of race as ordinarily conceived.

Andreasen (2005) counters Glasgow's (2003) objection to the cladistic race concept (and by extension to Kitcher's conception as well). Andreasen (2005, 98) argues that Glasgow's (2003) objection rests on a selective interpretation of the ordinary concept of race. Andreasen notes that historically, some racial classification schemes have relied principally on ancestry or genealogy at the expense of morphology. For instance, the one drop rule in the United States prioritizes ancestry in racializing individuals and groups. Furthermore, a study of the history of race conceptions shows that at one time or another anywhere from five to eight racial categories have been recognized in, for instance, the United States (Andreasen 2005, 100 f).

## 2.3 Races as Ecotypes

Massimo Pigliucci and Jonathan Kaplan (2003) argue that races are locally adapted ecotypes. Ecotypes are the result of selection pressure for ecologically important traits. The concept of ecotypes was initially developed to capture the genetic adaptation of plants (the latter also applied to animals) to their local environmental conditions (Pigliucci and Kaplan 2003, 1163). For instance, skin color is an ecologically significant adaptation. Lighter skin tones are adaptive in areas with low sunlight where the population is consuming a diet low in vitamin D (Pigliucci and Kaplan 2003, 1168). The crucial fact about ecotypes is that "adaptive genetic differentiation can be maintained between populations by natural selection even where there is significant gene flow between the populations" (1165). It is also possible for ecotypical traits to emerge independently in reproductively isolated populations undergoing the same selection pressure. Therefore, Pigliucci and Kaplan's account of race defends the biological basis of race while rejecting the view that races are phylogenetically distinct (contra Andreasen and Kitcher) or undergoing speciation.

---

[18] See the discussion of population stratification in Section 2.11.

However, as Pigliucci and Kaplan note, the ecotype concept of race has "little or nothing" to do with folk racial categories (1161). There are potentially dozens of ecotypes (i.e., local adaptations of smaller populations) including height, bone density, lung capacity, and so on. On the ecotype conception, these would constitute distinct races. Yet these traits are not commonly taken to be racial nor would the greater number of groups that fall under the ecotype conception be consistent with ordinary race. Of course, one can maintain that "race" has a "neutral" meaning that refers to the biological subdivisions of a species. Nonetheless, given the social and historical significance that "race" has, there is a high justificatory threshold to using "race" for a revisionist concept that is quite distinct from the ordinary usage.

So far, we have discussed biological conceptions of race which in one way or another diverge from the ordinary concept of race. Next, I discuss accounts of biological racial realism that are consistent with the ordinary race concept. This view has both *minimalist* and *robust* variants, with the view of races as genetic kinds the paradigmatic example of the latter.

## 2.4 Races as Genetic Kinds

Neven Sesardic (2000, 2010) defends a robust genetic view where races are distinct genetic groupings of human populations. Sesardic (2010) disputes the characterization of biological race realism used by its critics in order to dispute the biological reality of race. Sesardic admits that the overwhelming consensus among scientists (geneticists, anthropologists, etc.) as well as philosophers is that races are not biologically meaningful. However, Sesardic argues strong, essentialist assumptions are not necessary to ground a biological notion of race. If reasonable assumptions are made about what kinds of biological categories would count as "racial," then races can be "rescued" from debunking. Races in his account are not social or political, "racial recognition is not actually based on a single trait (like skin color) but rather on a number of characteristics that are to a certain extent concordant and that jointly make the classification not only possible but fairly reliable as well" (Sesardic 2010, 155). Sesardic claims that multifocal genetic clustering (that is, methodologies such as the one implemented by Rosenberg et al. 2002) reveals that race is a genetic category. Furthermore, genetic variation between races is what explains variation in hereditary traits, including psychological traits such as intelligence.

The robust view of biological racial realism has few defenders. It is out of step with the scientific consensus on the nature of human diversity (Long, Li, and Healy 2009; Rosenberg 2011; Biddanda, Rice, and Novembre 2020). It also draws on a contested view of the role of heredity in the development of complex traits. Sesardic's attempt to rescue folk races through the identification of races with genetic clusters misapplies the race concept (Hochman 2013). For one, if we specified races as populations with the least in group genetic variation, the resulting (hundreds of) clusters would fail to match any dominant conception of race or one that could reasonably be conceived of as one that picks out the ordinary concept. As Taylor notes, "if we delineated groups that had similar amounts of within-group genetic variation, most of the N groups would be in Africa" (Taylor 2011, 471).

## 2.5 Minimalist Biological Races

Recently, Michael O. Hardimon (2017a, 2017b), Quayshawn Spencer (2012, 2014, 2018), and Glasgow et al. (2019) have defended *minimalist* or *deflationary* accounts of race as biological. Their approach, which I call *minimalist biological racial realism,*[19] makes promising departures from previous accounts that defended a biological basis for race. Unlike revisionist biological conceptions of race, minimalist biological racial realism defends a view of biological races that captures the "logical core" of the ordinary race concept. While the view holds that races correspond to at least one structure of human genetic diversity, it rejects a robust interpretation of the genetic basis of race. Minimalist biological racial realism therefore holds that a conception of race consistent with the ordinary race concept is (i) biologically real and (ii) could end up, as a matter of empirical fact, not explaining a wide range of important genetic traits. Let us take each view in turn to see its strengths and, as I will argue, serious weaknesses.

For Hardimon (2017a, 2017b), it is possible to define a biologically genuine category that fulfills intuitive desiderata for a conception of race. Races, ordinarily conceived, are biological groups that vary from one another in physical characteristics such as skin color, eye shape, and lip form. Races are groups and "we can say that, for any given race R, there is an in-principle answer to the question, what pattern of visible physical characters does it exhibit?" (Hardimon 2017b, 151). Hardimon (2017b) provides the following definition of minimalist races: "a (minimalist) race is a group of human beings:

(1) which, as a group, is distinguished from other groups of human beings by patterns of visible physical features,

(2) whose members are linked by a common ancestry peculiar to members of the group, and which

(3) originates from a distinctive geographic location (Hardimon 2017b, 150).

---

[19] Although this is not what Spencer calls his view, as I discuss below Spencer's account has the defining features of minimalism.

Of course, it is trivial to construct categories that vary along some selected property. We could do so for height, weight, or any number of other biological or non-biological properties. Hardimon (2017b) defends the biological genuineness of races on three counts. First, the "patterns of visible physical features" that are the defining characteristic of races are biologically determined. There is a genetic and developmental basis for these varying traits. Second, as discussed above, genetic clustering algorithms such as *structure* used by Rosenberg and colleagues (2002) find a structure to human genetic diversity that, at $K = 5$, yields five continental populations that correspond to minimalist races. Third, there is an explanation both for why minimalist races have an underlying genetic structure and the variation in traits among minimalist races, namely, "biological raciation." As continental groups, minimalist races are geographically separate from one another and are separately subject to founder effects and genetic drift. Furthermore, the salient racial features such as skin color are plausibly adaptations to the different ecological pressures. Hardimon argues that "minimalist race counts as biologically significant because a number of its visible physical features such as skin color are almost certainly evolutionary adaptations to the climate of the aboriginal home of the minimalist races" (Hardimon 2017b, 158). Taken together, Hardimon (2017b) argues these three facts show that minimalist races are a biologically meaningful category.

Hardimon rejects the unsound inferences of the essentialist biological race conception. Minimalist races are not claimed to have normative or further genetic significance. Minimalist race is biological merely because the physical features that classify races – lip form, eye shape, skin color – are biological traits and geographic ancestry is a biologically relevant distinction. Furthermore, physical differences do not tell us anything about underlying genetic diversity other than perhaps about the genetic and developmental source of those differences. That is, there may be a great deal of genetic diversity between populations that show no salient physical differences, and vice versa. The genetic pathways that determine outward traits are a tiny fraction of the overall genome.

Quayshawn Spencer (2012, 2014, 2018) and Glasgow et al. (2019) defend the biological reality of race along similar lines to Hardimon. Spencer's account is both revisionist and minimalist. It is revisionist because Spencer takes "race" not be a kind but an entity. Specifically, on Spencer's account race refers to a set of human populations. The account is minimalist because Spencer does not take race to be robustly explanatory in the way race essentialism does. For Spencer, to say that race is biologically real is to hold that it is "an epistemically useful and justified entity in a well-ordered research program in biology, which I will call a genuine biological entity" (Glasgow et al. 2019, 95).[20] That is, race has the same status as "monophyletic group, TYRP1 gene, hypothalamus," which are cases of good scientific classification. These are rivaled by cases of bad scientific classification, such as "gemmule, baramin, and destructiveness organ" (Spencer 2012, 185), which scientists would reject.

Spencer (2012) argues that the feature that genuine entities share is that they advance long-term scientific progress. The genuine entities promote "*epistemic progress in science, such as improving our ability to predict known phenomena, or accurately predicting novel phenomena*" (Spencer 2012, 186). Genuine entities play an epistemic role in a well-ordered scientific research program. They are fruitful and lead scientists down exploratory paths that are likely to lead to new discoveries instead of dead ends. In the case of biology, Spencer argues that $e$ is a genuine biological entity if,

(i) $e$ is useful for generating a theory t in a biological research program p,
(ii) using $e$ to generate t is warranted according to the epistemic values of p to explain or predict an observational law of p, and
(iii) p has coherent and well-motivated aims, competitive predictive power, and frequent cross-checks (Spencer 2012, 193).

Spencer argues that each of these conditions is satisfied in the case of race. Condition (iii) is fulfilled by population genetics, which is one of the core research programs of biology. As for the first two conditions, Spencer argues that research into human population structure and genetic clustering algorithms by Rosenberg and colleagues (2002) and latter researchers vindicate the biological genuineness of race. A species can be subdivided into a number of populations, where K is the number of populations. These divisions are the population structure of the species. As we have seen, at $K = 5$, we get the human continental populations: Africans, Eurasians, East Asians, Native Americans, and Oceanians. These human continental populations, Spencer argues, satisfy conditions (ii) because, they successfully generate a theory about human population structure in which the "observational law is that humans have $K = 5$ genetic structure that is largely geographically clustered in the following regions: the Americas, Sub-Saharan Africa, Oceania, Eurasia east of the Himalayas, and Eurasia west of the Himalayas and North Africa" (Glasgow et al. 2019, 99). That is, as Rosenberg and colleagues (2002) have shown, the human continental populations are the population subdivision obtained by *structure* at $K = 5$. Furthermore, Spencer argues that these human continental

---

[20] Spencer (2012) had referred to them as genuine *kinds*. I use his latter language (i.e., entity) throughout.

populations are *identical* to at least one scheme of racial classification, namely, the US Office of Management and Budget's (OMB) 1997 racial categories: Black or African, White, American Indian or Alaska Native, and Native Hawaiian or Other Pacific Islander. Therefore, given that human continental populations are biologically real, OMB races (which are identical to these populations) are biologically real.

Crucially for Spencer, even though races are genuine biological entities, "the only metaphysical fact that follows from a [entity] being genuine is that it is *real enough* to use in ongoing scientific research" (Spencer 2012, 194). Spencer's biological racial realism is therefore minimalist. The account does not ground the biological genuineness of race in the fact that race explains a vast array of biological, psychological, or other phenomena. Rather, by fulfilling the conditions of realness or genuineness, it *could* play an explanatory role in scientific research programs such as medical genetics. As Glasgow et al. puts it, "we now know that it's metaphysically possible for some races to matter in medical genetics because some races are biologically real" (Glasgow et al. 2019, 104). Because OMB race is biologically real, it is metaphysically possible that race matters in medical genetics. It is "real enough" to be explanatorily or predictively useful. However, Glasgow et al. notes:

> OMB race theory does not *imply* that OMB races differ in medically relevant allele frequencies, and it does not imply that OMB races *don't* differ in medically relevant allele frequencies. Likewise, OMB race theory does not imply that OMB races differ in any socially important traits (e.g., intelligence, beauty, moral character, etc.), and it does not imply that OMB races don't differ in any socially important traits. Determining whether OMB races differ in any phenotypic ways requires a separate empirical investigation. (Glasgow et al. 2019, 104)

This is what makes Spencer's view minimalist. The biological reality of race does not depend on the fact that it robustly explains a wide range of empirical phenomena. In fact, it may turn out, after empirical investigation, that there is no other way OMB races differ phenotypically than in the defining racial traits. But that is neither here nor there on whether races are biologically real. It is possible that races matter explanatorily because they are real, they are not real because they are (robustly) explanatory.

In summary, Spencer and Hardimon defend a minimalist biological racial realism that captures key elements of the ordinary concept of race. What makes their accounts minimalist is that they eschew the inference from biological race to the clustering of other significant biological properties (aside from those that are defining physical characteristics of races). They claim, rather, that it is possible for a minimalist biological race to be useful in biology. The main candidate for the epistemic usefulness of biological race is medicine. In the next section, I discuss criticism of minimalist biological racial realism.

## 2.6 Are Minimal Races Biological?

Eric Winsberg (2022) argues that Spencer's approach represents the best attempt thus far to ground race in biology, but nonetheless fails. Winsberg argues that the connection Spencer draws between human continental populations, distinguishability by *structure*-like programs, and the OMB races cannot sustain the conclusion that races are biologically real entities. First, Winsberg argues, human continental populations are not biological entities. As discussed in Section 2.5, Spencer (2018) drew on two facts to defend the claim human continental populations are biologically real: human continental populations are distinguishable by *structure*-like programs and we can explain why they are so distinguished by appeal to evolutionary forces such as drift, selection, and mutation. For instance, Spencer (2018) claims Native Americans are "modified descendants" of Northeast Asians. They are "modified" through changes induced by evolutionary forces. These changes are what explain why Native Americans are a distinct genetic cluster identified by *structure*.

Winsberg (2022) denies that it is the genetic clustering of *present-day* Native Americans that facilitates structure-like programs' ability to pick them out is the product of evolutionary forces. Rather, the explanation for why such clustering exists after the age of discovery has to cite "the complex social history of racial segregation that has preserved this clustering over five centuries of colonial and post-colonial history" (Winsberg 2022, 13). After all, we might add, an "Indian reservation" is not a barrier erected by nature. As such, it is not clear why human continental populations are *biological* entities if they are (currently) maintained primarily by *social* mechanisms of isolation and cohesion. They may be real *scientific* kinds, but they are not biological. More crucially, Winsberg (2022) argues that even if we are warranted in holding population subdivisions are real scientific kinds, it does not follow that each and every population subdivision constitutes a real kind. We can hold that *color* is a real kind without committing ourselves to the claim that *green* or *yellow* or *wine-dark red* are real kinds. Consequently, it is possible that structure-like programs discover real scientific kinds that are integral to the success of population genetics. Nonetheless, it does not follow that any given cluster discovered by *structure* is a real scientific kind, let alone a biological one.

Furthermore, Winsberg (2022) rejects the claim that OMB races are identical to human continental populations. As Winsberg (2022) observes, the Census Bureau uses the OMB racial classification scheme to roughly operationalize a (murky) social notion of race prevailing in the United States. How does this highly qualified approach produce categories that end up being *identical* to races qua biological entities? It is all the more puzzling since Spencer's claim is not that the OMB races are merely contingently coextensive with biological races. Spencer rather holds that the OMB races *refer* to the human continental populations, which are in turn biological entities. Winsberg (2022) argues the five OMB racial groups are not picked out referentially. The five OMB racial groups are not rigid designators, they do not have fixed references. The social process in which the OMB races were formulated was highly contingent and is even now subject to change. It would be a massive coincidence, one that Spencer leaves unexplained, if the OMB races came to robustly identify biological populations.

## 2.7 Minimalist Biological Race and the Gerrymandering Objection

The objections Winsberg (2022) raises to Spencer are a consequence of a broader issue with minimalist biological racial realism. Namely, their approach attempts to show how our murky, contingent, and contested social notion of race, or at least a conception consistent with one version of it, is also part of the biological structure of the world. I argue that minimalist or OMB races fail to count as genuine *biological* kinds or entities. Spencer (2012) and Glasgow et al. (2019) are right that for races to be biologically real they need not fulfill stringent criteria such as being independent from scientific interests or fundamental categories of population genetics. Many accounts ground biological realness (or biological naturalness) in the perspectives, interests, and practices of scientists (see Kitcher 2007). However, the fact that races according to at least one classification scheme correspond to population structure in humans is not sufficient to establish that races are biologically real or genuine. At least not in the way "hypothalamus" or "TYRP1 gene" are genuinely biological. I argue this is because minimalist biological racial realism is confronted by a dilemma. Either, as a matter of empirical fact, race explains very little or nothing in biology, in which case this gives rise to the gerrymandering objection against minimalist biological races; or race is robustly explanatory in biological sciences, in which case minimalism would have to be abandoned in favor of a robustly realist position.

On the first horn, the minimalist realist is confronted by the gerrymandering objection which holds that minimalist biological races are gerrymandered kinds or entities. The distinction between natural or genuine kinds and properties on the one hand and unnatural or pathological kinds or properties on the other is at the forefront of metaphysics and philosophy of science. David Lewis' (1983) groundbreaking "New Work for a Theory of Universals" highlighted the centrality of naturalness in theories of explanation, laws of nature, similarity, and induction, among others. Furthermore, any scientific project involving categorization or classification needs a principle by which to distinguish appropriate from inappropriate classifications, regardless of how pluralist the account (Franklin-Hall 2015). Classificatory practice in science has to be disciplined by a carving principle that tracks the grooves and joints of nature. As Franklin-Hall (2015) writes, "thus we do well or badly, classification-wise, to the extent that our partitions track the kinds embedded in nature itself, and the pathological categories are those that in no way – even but through a glass darkly – match the world's own" (Franklin-Hall 2015, 926).

Gerrymandering objections charge that a proposed entity or kind is inappropriately "built up". To be gerrymandered is one way a kind or entity can lack naturalness or genuineness. There are many accounts of metaphysical naturalness or genuineness, and I do not discuss here the considerable literature on metaphysical naturalness. Nonetheless, there are certain desiderata that are widely held as integral to naturalness. I discuss two core features that minimalist races lack that render them liable to the gerrymandering objection. First, natural kinds or properties are projectible or portable. There is no consensus on how to characterize projectability.[21] The basic idea is that projectability makes inductive inferences permissible. For a natural kind $S$, we can legitimately infer from X is $S$ to other predicates in relation to which it is projectible (Khalidi 2018, 1380 f). For instance, in Goodman's ([1955]/1983) classic example, we can project from X is an *emerald* to X is *green*. One of the telltale signs that an entity or kind is gerrymandered is a lack of projectability or explanatory connection to a wide range of explananda-phenomena.

I argue that biological races (minimally conceived) are not projectible or portable. As such, they do not possess an explanatorily or epistemically privileged status such as realness or genuineness. And this is partly because they have been *minimally* conceived. By the lights of Hardimon and Spencer themselves, it is possible biological races do not explain a wide range of phenomena, although they maintain it possible that they may do so. I do not claim that there is nothing that minimalist races explain. After all, the fact that minimalist races correspond to genetic clusters at $K = 5$ in Rosenberg and colleagues' (2002) model means that minimalist races can explain facts about the distinctness of those clusters. And racial traits such as skin color are biological traits explained by biological mechanisms. Hardimon and Spencer draw on these

---

[21] See Goodman ([1955]/1983) for an influential early characterization of projectability. Khalidi (2018) defends an account more suited to sciences where laws or universal generalizations play little to no role.

facts to ground their realism. But the limited explanatory role is not enough to avoid a gerrymandering objection. Gerrymandered kinds or entities are also capable of explaining some phenomena. Take for instance Fodor's (1974, 11) example of a manifestly unnatural kind, the kind *is transported to a distance of less than three miles from the Eiffel Tower.* Let's call this kind $T$. There are things that $T$ predicts and explains. For instance, for goods sold in shops, $T$ explains why they are denominated in Euros. It predicts that they are likely to be more expensive than other goods sold in France. It may explain other things besides. Nonetheless, $T$ has extremely limited portability. It does not figure into robust explanatory relations of the kind sought by sciences. Furthermore, whatever $T$ explains is *better explained* by other, more natural kinds.

Second, and relatedly, natural kinds or properties contribute to scientific understanding. Scientific fields are interested in or investigate kinds that are maximally mutually explanatory with respect to the target regularities studied by that science. Physical kinds such as *charge, spin, charm, field,* and so on and neurobiological kinds such as, *neuron, neurotransmitter, synapse,* and so on have respective robust explanatory connections that facilitate understanding how the regularities studied by a given science (fundamental physics, neuroscience) fit together (Bhogal, 2023). Minimalist races lack these valuable explanatory connections in biology that would justify their biological naturalness or genuineness. Note that, for instance, Kitcher's revisionist race conception does not face the same challenge. Kitcher (2007) begins by explicitly drawing on the standard biological practice in apportioning populations, namely, the division of species and subspecies. On Kitcher's approach, if "race" is a biological subdivision of the human species, it should be characterized in the same way other biological subspecies are. This approach has the potential to yield explanatory connections between "race" and a cluster of explananda-phenomena in humans as subspecies have to their respective clusters in other species.

The (potential) explanatory value of revisionist biological conceptions of race may have come at the price of abandoning commitment to the ordinary race concept. In so far as the minimalist conception is of an ordinary race concept, it will fail to pick out an explanatorily relevant kind or entity *in biology.* As Long, Li, and Healy (2009) conclude in their study of race and genetic diversity:

> The pattern of DNA sequence diversity also creates some unsettling problems for applying to humans the definition of races as groups of populations within which the individuals are more related to each other than they are to members of other such groups . . . A classification that takes into account evolutionary relationships and the nested pattern of diversity would require that Sub-Saharan Africans are not a race because the most exclusive group that includes all Sub-Saharan African populations also includes every non-Sub-Saharan African population.

Moreover, the Out-of-Africa branch would place all Eurasians in the same race, but this would necessitate placing Europeans and Asians in sub-races. Several sub-sub-races would be necessary to account for the population groups throughout the world. We see no need for such a classification in light of the fact that our evolutionary history gives good guidance for understanding the structure of human diversity. (Long, Li, and Healy 2009, 32–33)

Human genetic diversity tracks patterns of human population dispersal and local population dynamics that are out of sync with the ordinary race concept.

I have argued that minimalist races are liable to a gerrymandering objection. But this is the case only if minimalist races fail to explain a wide range of phenomena. And that is in fact the case. Minimalist races are not projectible or portable; they do limited explanatory work in biology. Some of what they explain is better explained by other subdivisions of humans at a higher or lower grain (Kalewold 2020). Minimalist races therefore do not advance biological understanding. Race *minimally biologically conceived* lacks the constraints to count as among the biological kinds along with TYRP1 gene, monophyletic group, and hypothalamus (all of which are robustly explanatorily connected to other genuine kinds and the regularities they underlie or produce). The gerrymandering objection would be weak if it held race to a higher standard than other biologically genuine or natural kinds. However, it is by looking at other biological kinds that we can see how minimalist races fail to secure the kind of value necessary for *biological* naturalness. To see why, let us turn to a discussion of dimensions of explanatory value in biology.

## 2.8 Explanatory Value in Biology

Jim Woodward (2010) discusses three dimensions of explanatory value in the biological sciences; stability, specificity, and proportionality (Woodward 2010, 292). To take just one of these values briefly, Woodward (2010) develops specificity by (i) drawing on Lewis' notion of influence and (ii) the one-to-one conception of causation. Specificity is often invoked to account for the privileged role DNA plays in explaining the development of various phenotypes. Woodward (2010) argues that the best way to conceive of specificity, and the special causal role of DNA, is as a form of fine-grained influence. According to influence, "C will influence E to the extent that by varying the state of C and its time and place of occurrence, we can modulate the state of E in a fine-grained way" (Woodward 2010, 305). Woodward (2010) illustrates influence with an analogy to a dial on a radio. Moving the dial on a radio will change the stations in a fine-grained way and a given position of the dial is associated with a particular radio station (307). Causal relationships that lack specificity on the other hand are more switch-like.

Whether the radio is plugged in or not for instance is not causally specific since it does not have fine-grained influence on the operations of the radio. It is in this sense that DNA is distinct from the other "cellular machinery" in causing various phenotypes. Changes in RNA polymerases, ribosomes, and energy molecules (ATP, GTP) do not have fine-grained influence over the product. However, in the case of DNA, "there are many possible states of the DNA sequence and many (although not all) variations in this sequence are systematically associated with different possible corresponding states of the linear sequences of the mRNA molecules and of the proteins synthesized" (306).

Woodward (2010) considers a second standard for specificity, which sees specificity as approximating a one cause–one effect relationship. This notion of specificity draws on epidemiology where identifying a one-to-one relationship between a cause and a disease effect is the gold standard of epidemiological research. For instance, cases where being exposed to a particular toxin causes one disease, or a specific gene variant causes one disorder, and so on. Of course, most diseases have a many cause–many effect causal relationship and do not fit the one-to-one standard. Woodward (2010) amends this notion by marking it not as a criterion of causation, but as a biologically significant type of causal relationship. In this sense of specificity, "$C$ will be a more (rather than less) specific cause (in the one-to-one sense) to the extent that it causes only a few different kinds of effects within a pre-specified range" (311). For example, enzyme activity is more specific if it interacts with only a narrow range of substrates and produces only a limited number of effects. Specificity is an important dimension of explanatory value for biology. Biologists do not merely look for any entity or kind and its relationship to the target they wish to explain. As discussed by Woodward (2010), it is the specific (causal) explanatory relations, and the entities that engage with them, that are of scientific interest to biologists.

The problem for minimalist or OMB races is that they are at an inappropriate grain to secure explanatory value in biology. In order for minimalist races to have explanatory value *in biology*, what we would want to see is *specific, robust, and proportional* explanatory relations between minimalist races and the regularities they (possibly) explain. Consider a contrast case such as enzyme action. The core properties of an enzyme – its size, shape, and configuration – are what explains its derivative properties including its binding, affinities, and so on. In the case of minimalist race, however, what explains biogenetic phenomena that seemingly vary racially, such as the incidence of genetic diseases such as sickle cell disease and lactose intolerance, or even defining physical characteristics such as skin color are not explanatorily connected to race *per se*. There is no *specific* explanatory relation between race and these other properties (see the following subsections).[22]

Additionally, the minimalist biological race concept takes continental barriers to be a core driver of (genetic) distinctiveness between races. Human population genetics research vindicates at least a deflationary view of what that distinctiveness amounts to. Nonetheless, geographic distance as a result of continental barriers is not the only kind of barrier that is sufficient to establish population structure. For instance, linguistic differences between geographically co-located populations are sufficient for reproductive isolation (Hellwege et al. 2017). Population stratification therefore occurs at a much smaller, and more local, scale than the continental. As Hellwege and colleagues note "allele frequencies change randomly over time as an independent process for each population isolate, ultimately causing observable differences in the frequency of many alleles after several generations of separation and differentiation" (Hellwege et al. 2017, 2). Sophisticated clustering algorithms are capable of distinguishing between dozens or hundreds of population groups. For instance, Gao and Starmer (2007) debuted a clustering program capable of identifying clusters that differentiate between Chinese and Japanese populations (Gao and Starmer 2007). What population stratification showed was that other clusterings of human populations were also distinct and potentially explanatorily more relevant in explaining medical and other phenomena. They act on populations within and across different putatively biological (ordinary) races.

To motivate this objection, I consider the most widely cited candidate for the explanatory usefulness of race to science – medical genetics.

## 2.9 The Case of Race and Medical Genetics

The gerrymandering objection to minimalist biological races charges that they lack essential dimensions of explanatory value. For instance, in order to be

---

[22] For instance, the dark skin of Australian aborigines and Sub-Saharan Africans is a result of selection pressure. However, it does not reflect proximate biogeographic ancestry. On the contrary, Eurasians with lighter skin color are biogeographically closer to Africans than Australian aborigines (Rasmussen et al. 2011). As Pigliucci and Kaplan (2003) note, "similar skin color [. . .] represents not a shared ancestry but rather similar selective pressures" (Pigliucci and Kaplan 2003, 1168). In fact, even within the same continent ecotypical traits emerge independently in reproductively distant populations. Hardimon may avoid this problem by reiterating that minimalist races are not meant to have sharp boundaries. But here again we see the intuitive basis of the defining conditions of minimalist race on the one hand and population genetics and the science of human origins on the other coming apart. The explanation of the rise of adaptive traits among populations as they dispersed across the world may appeal to *raciation*, but it does not need to. In fact, appeal to races may obscure the mechanisms and selection pressure responsible (see the discussion in Section 2.9 about race and medical genetics). There is, therefore, no robust explanatory relation between (potentially) adaptive physical features such as skin color on the one hand, and geography and ancestry on the other.

explanatorily apt in medical genetics, the genetic variation at the level of racial category must correspond to variation in rates of disease incidence characterized at that level (specificity). The racial categories must secure an epidemiological explanatory value that is missing either at higher (species) or lower (local population) organizational levels. As Root (2003) argues, this matching of the appropriate grain is one they fail to achieve (Root 2003). Genetic studies must demonstrate a causal-explanatory relationship between "medically relevant" genes that vary racially and disease-phenomena. Yet, the examples commonly cited by biological racial realists, such as lactase persistence and sickle cell anemia (Spencer 2018), fail to demonstrate the explanatory value of biological race. To see why, let's look at these cases in turn.

## 2.10 Sickle Cell Disease

Consider the explanation for the prevalence of sickle cell anemia in sub-Saharan Africa, a commonly cited candidate for a disease in which race is a medically relevant category. Sickle cell anemia (HbSS) is a severe form of the inherited red blood cell disorder called SCD. As the name suggests, patients with SCD have abnormal rigid and sickle-shaped hemoglobin (i.e., red blood cells). Healthy hemoglobin is disc-shaped and flexible, permitting easy movement through blood vessels. Abnormal hemoglobin (Hb) on the other hand has a rigid, sickle-like structure that, among other things, makes them prone to snag on the walls of blood vessels leading to restricted blood flow and other serious symptoms such as pain, blindness, and stroke.

Sickle cell disease is a genetic disorder. Patients with SCD have inherited a gene that codes for abnormal hemoglobin from each parent.[23] In the case of sickle cell anemia, patients have inherited sickle (HbS) hemoglobin gene from both parents. Sickle cell trait is a heterozygous form of SCD where the patient inherits a normal hemoglobin gene from one parent and an abnormal hemoglobin (such as *HBB* or HbC) from the other. While sickle cell anemia is a debilitating disease, individuals with sickle cell trait are usually healthy and do not present with the serious symptoms of other SCD (Piel, Steinberg, and Rees 2017).

---

[23] The most common forms of sickle cell disease are sickle cell anemia, sickle cell hemoglobin C disease, sickle cell beta-plus-thalassemia (Sβ+), and sickle cell beta-zero-thalassemia (Sβ0). Sickle cell hemoglobin C disease (SC) is caused by one copy of the sickle cell mutation and one copy of the hemoglobin C mutation (HbC). Sickle cell beta-plus-thalassemia (Sβ+) is caused by one copy of the sickle cell mutation and one copy of a mutation in the beta-globin gene that reduces beta-globin production. Sickle cell beta-zero-thalassemia (Sβ0) is caused by two copies of a beta-globin mutation that completely eliminates beta-globin production, in combination with one copy of the sickle cell mutation (Piel, Steinberg, and Rees 2017).

The prevalence of a debilitating genetic disorder like sickle cell anemia in any population is striking given the putative selection pressure against it. The explanation for this puzzling phenomenon is now well-known and has to do with the fact that sickle cell trait provides protection from malaria. This in turn explains its relative prevalence in sub-Saharan Africa, the Middle East, the Mediterranean Basin, and India: all regions with high levels of endemic malaria. There are two distinct explanations linking the sickle cell trait to malaria: (1) a mechanistic explanation of how the sickle cell trait neutralizes the *plasmodium* parasite that causes malaria, and (2) the evolutionary explanation of how the variant responsible for this trait is preserved in the affected populations.

How then does race come into the explanatory picture of sickle cell anemia? The mechanistic explanation of how sickle cell trait protects from malaria does not depend on nor inform facts about race.[24] The evolutionary explanation of the prevalence of sickle cell disease is tied to the protection from malaria provided by the sickle cell trait. Individuals who carry one copy of the sickle cell allele and one copy of the normal hemoglobin allele have a selective advantage over individuals who have two copies of the normal hemoglobin allele or two copies of the sickle cell allele. The selective advantage arises because individuals with sickle cell trait are more resistant to malaria than those with normal hemoglobin, but they do not suffer from the severe symptoms of sickle cell disease that are associated with having two copies of the sickle cell allele. This results in the selection for balanced polymorphism in malaria-affected populations (Allison 2002; Piel, Steinberg, and Rees 2017).

Although sickle cell disease is particularly associated with sub-Saharan Africa, and with African Americans in the United States, it is also present in other regions with endemic malaria. As Williams and Weatherall note, "sickle cell anemia occurs throughout sub-Saharan Africa and in small pockets in the Mediterranean region, the Middle East, and the Indian subcontinent" (Williams and Weatherall 2012, 1). The sickle cell gene arose independently at least twice, once in and once out of Africa. Since the selection pressure is due to endemic malaria, it is unsurprising that other malarial geographic regions also show the prevalence of sickle cell trait. Although sickle cell anemia produced by the

---

[24] In brief, the mechanism is as follows: sickle hemoglobin releases free heme into the plasma at higher levels than normal hemoglobin. Free heme in turn induce HO-1 expression, which prevents the toxicity of free heme. The HO-1 mechanism by which free heme toxicity is counteracted has a beneficial side effect. Namely, the metabolism of free heme by HO-1 produces (non-toxic) amounts of carbon monoxide (CO). CO inhibits the release of free heme by stabilizing the quaternary structure of hemoglobin, which prevents it from dissociating into its toxic subunits. The suppression of free heme deprives plasmodium of a crucial component of malaria pathogenesis (Ferreira et al. 2011, 401–405). Other metabolic products of HO-1 potentially also play a protective role against malaria.

sickle hemoglobin allele (HbS) is widely identified as a disease affecting "African Americans," there is considerable heterogeneity in its incidence within the putative minimalist black or OMB "Black or African American" race. As Allison (2002) shows, "among tribes living close to the coast of Kenya or to Lake Victoria, the frequencies exceeded 20%, whereas among several tribes living in the Kenyan highlands or in arid country, the frequencies were less than 1%. These differences cut across linguistic and cultural boundaries and were independent of blood group markers that we documented" (Allison 2002, 280). The source of this heterogeneity is the differential prevalence of malaria. Piel and colleagues (2010) found "the gradual increase in HbS allele frequencies from epidemic areas to holoendemic areas in Africa is consistent with the hypothesis that malaria protection by HbS involves the enhancement of not only innate but also acquired immunity" (Piel et al. 2010, 3).

Given that the African ancestors of African Americans were predominantly drawn from malaria-prone regions, they unsurprisingly have higher rates of sickle cell disease and other "genetic variants that confer resistance to malaria are associated with RBC [red blood cell] traits in African-Americans" (Ding et al. 2013, 1061). However, the social and political history of where the African ancestors of African Americans originated is once again not a fact that is connected to *biological* races. The evolutionary lineages of *local* population groups across multiple continents, and the distinct selection pressure that led to the prevalence of sickle cell alleles that are adaptive in those specific malaria-prone environments, specifically and proportionally explain why these populations disproportionately suffer from sickle cell anemia. Minimalist or OMB races do not come into the explanatory picture in a valuable way.

## 2.11 Lactase Persistence

A second commonly cited example of the relevance of a genetic race concept to medicine is the case of lactase persistence (Spencer 2018, 1028). Lactase persistence refers to the ability to digest lactose in adulthood. It is a genetic trait that has evolved in humans in response to the domestication and exploitation of dairy animals. While lactose intolerance is the norm in most human populations, the frequency of lactase persistence varies widely across different populations, with the highest frequencies found in populations that historically relied on milk as a source of nutrition, such as in northern Europe, and lower frequencies found in populations that did not have a tradition of milk consumption, such as in East Asia and parts of Africa. The absence of lactase persistence (LP) before the bronze and iron ages and the subsequent explosion of LP suggests LP is one of the strongest cases of positive selection in recent human evolutionary history (Evershed et al. 2022).

The evolutionary explanation of lactase persistence is one example of how human biology and culture have coevolved over time. Although LP selection must be related to milk consumption, the exact mechanism by which LP contributes to inclusive fitness is not fully understood. Evershed and colleagues (2022) find that LP is not associated with higher milk consumption. Rather, individuals with LP fare better during contingent adverse events such as famine. The ability to digest milk confers an advantage during these adverse events, driving LP selection (Evershed et al. 2022). In any case, there is nothing racial (or continental) about the explanation of the rise of LP. It acts on populations on the basis of their dietary choices and other environmental factors, which vary both within and across continents. Nothing at the vast population grain of *race* plays a specific or robust explanatory role.

## 2.12 Population Stratification

The upshot of the discussion in previous sections is that race, as a biological population, entity, or kind, is not part of the productive continuity of genetic racial disparities in sickle cell disease or lactase persistence. That is, race qua biological is not robustly explanatorily connected to these genetic traits in a way that secured explanatory value. Of course, this is not to deny that population-level genetic differences can play an explanatory role in medicine. Rather, the population in question is only rarely racial. Given the factors that produce genetic diversity between continental populations – reproductive isolation, selection, genetic drift – also operate at a much finer grain, it would be a massive coincidence if it were racial difference,[25] as opposed to populational differences at a different grain, that accounted for a large share of epidemiological difference.

This problem is general and not specific to the two medical cases discussed in Sections 2.10 and 2.11. The investigative tool used to investigate the connection between genetics and epidemiological racial disparities, namely, GWAS studies, is limited in its ability to secure the explanatory value or biological races.

Genome-Wide Association Studies (GWAS) are a set of tools drawn from population genetics used to identify statistical relationships between single-nucleotide polymorphisms (SNPs) and phenotypic traits. An SNP is a nucleotide, at a particular locus on a chromosome, that varies across individuals. Genome Wide Association Studies (GWAS) scan the genome of suitably

---

[25] Of course, a specifically racial explanation might be called for in contexts where racism or social race are the most robust explanans. But these are not biological accounts of race.

defined groups to identify whether there is SNP variation (e.g., a group of individuals with Multiple Sclerosis and a control group of individuals without the disease). GWAS studies are at the forefront of research into the relationship between genotypes and diseases. The GWAS Catalog includes GWAS studies that have found over 50,000 significant associations between genetic variants and diseases and traits (Tam 2019). Nevertheless, GWAS studies do not indicate whether these associations are causal or spurious, or whether the implicated SNPs are actually involved in the pathogenesis of the diseases with which they are associated.

GWAS studies on epidemiological racial disparities attempt to identify SNPs associated with a disease phenotype within human subpopulations. However, there are limitations to the explanatory value of the statistical associations revealed by GWAS into epidemiological racial disparities. For instance, GWAS studies are constrained by a population stratification (PS) problem (Hellwege et al. 2017). PS is a significant limitation on the robustness of GWAS' association identification. PS is a result of nonrandom mating "due to geographic isolation of subpopulations with low rates of migration and gene flow over the course of several generations" (Hellwege et al. 2017, 2). This isolation is not caused solely by continental barriers but also as a result of linguistic, cultural, or other barriers to free and random mating. In the absence of a random distribution of alleles, GWAS studies need to account for this underlying stratification in order to avoid spurious correlations. As Hellwege and colleagues (2017) show, "the differentiation among subpopulations is detectable even when the regional differences are subtle, as has been described in Chinese and Japanese and European populations [. . .] Cultural differences among populations also create stratification, even when populations inhabit the same geographical region" (Hellwege et al. 2017, 3).

The consequence of population stratification is not that more powerful tools will fail to overcome these challenges and yield meaningful results. Rather, the nature of population stratification reveals that local populations are a biologically significant element of the human genetic mosaic. Of course, arguing that race is meaningfully biological does not preclude the reality of subracial populations and vice versa. However, the fact that criteria such as distinguishability are applicable to a far larger number of population groups implies it would be a massive coincidence if the racial level turned out to be explanatorily apt across a range of explananda-phenomena. Indeed, as Hou and colleagues (2023) find in their research on the causal contribution of differing ancestry in admixed (i.e., multiple ancestry) individuals such as African Americans, there is "minimal heterogeneity in causal effects by ancestry."

Race (as the realist conceives it) figures into far fewer explanatory relations than the more fine-grained local populations of which it is composed. As such, (minimalist or OMB) race is an explanatory orphan in biology. To say that minimalist biological races are explanatory orphans is to hold that they fail to secure an explanatory value that is missing at a higher or lower populational grain. Explanatory accuracy is relatively trivial to obtain for categories. Strevens (2008), for instance, notes that we can disjunctively create a causal model to explain some target phenomenon which is accurate but nonetheless inappropriate. In his example, he asks us to consider two causal models for Rasputin's death, one involving his drowning due to being bound and thrown in a river (influviation) and another his poisoning. Suppose that it is the influviation, rather than the poisoning, that is a difference-maker for his death. Then an accurate explanation of Rasputin's death will cite the fact that Rasputin was bound and thrown in the river as the explanans. We can go further and "take the disjunction of the setups of the two models and form a new model that has the disjunction as its setup: it states that *either* Rasputin was thrown in a river *or* he was fed poison teacakes, and so on. The disjunctive model is veridical, since one of these chains of events did occur as claimed, and it entails Rasputin's death, since both chains of events lead to death" (Strevens 2008, 102). However, the disjunctive model is gerrymandered. In Strevens' (2008) account, it lacks *cohesion*. The ability to generate gerrymandered entities or models that nonetheless are explanatorily accurate is a major impetus for accounts of naturalness or genuineness. Explanations that cite gerrymandered entities might be accurate, but they will lack explanatory value.

In summary, I argue that what matters in establishing the genuineness of *biological* kinds or entities is whether they participate robustly in biological explanatory practice. The factors that are supposed to secure the genuine biological kindness of minimalist race – adaptiveness, distinguishability, and so on – are readily applicable to larger or smaller population groups that secure dimensions of explanatory value (proportionality, robustness, stability, and so on) that minimalist races lack. Distinguishability, as measured by *structure*-like programs, is possible for other possible groupings. Indeed, given enough sites, it is possible to detect population structure down to the level of families. Given the discussion in this section, it raises the question of why a race-based model would be favored in biomedical research. As Glasgow et al. (2019, 115) notes:

> On the assumption that the goal is to organize ourselves into meaningful (or potentially meaningful) biological categories for the purposes of medical research, wouldn't a more fine-grained (or differently grained) classification system be better? Why not divide up human populations along the lines of historical exposure to malaria (so linked to sickle cell disease), or those

descended from pastoral tribes (so less prone to lactose intolerance), or annual exposure to sunlight (relevant to vitamin D absorption and other diseases such as multiple sclerosis), or many other possible classifications? Given that the state can undertake to enforce just about any system, why shouldn't the OMB use a more obviously biologically fruitful one? Or why include racial categories on the census (and other legal documents) at all and instead leave the classification to the medical professionals?

And because these different grains will be more explanatorily valuable, (minimalist biological) races do not figure into more robust, more specific, or more stable explanations than explanations that cite other human populations.

Of course, for all I have said, minimalist or OMB races can be real in some other metaphysical sense. They may be *socially* real (see the next section). Or they may be *basic* or *primitive*. For instance, Glasgow et al. (2019) proposes a "basic" racial realism. Glasgow et al. (2019) proposes that race is possibly real in a basic metaphysical sense that is not grounded in either biological or social facts. Race is basic in this sense because it is outside the purview of science (Glasgow et al. 2019, 139). As an illustration of the kind of thing a race could be, Glasgow et al. (2019) gives the example of *sundogs*, where S is a *sundog* if it is either a sun or a dog. Even if *sundogs* play no role in science, they may still nonetheless exist. Glasgow et al. (2019) write that "barring a radical change in the universe, you'll never see sundogs show up in a biology or sociology textbook. Nevertheless, it sure looks like there are things that are either suns or dogs. Fido is a sundog, because Fido is a dog. So it is plausible to say that sundogs are real, even if they are scientifically irrelevant" (Glasgow et al. 2019, 139). Glasgow calls things like sundogs basic kinds. And race is possibly one such kind.

Glasgow et al.'s (2019) basic racial realism is not liable to the gerrymandering objection in so far as he readily admits that it is gerrymandered. Furthermore, because it is gerrymandered, as Glasgow et al. (2019) note, it is inappropriate to use in scientific theorizing. The charge I make against minimalist biological racial realism is that minimalist races are also gerrymandered. Their grounding in biology is superficial. The biological races they defend fail to secure explanatory values that are central to the life sciences. After all, it is metaphysically possible that even *sundogs* could play an explanatory role in science. But they would fail to be good or valuable explanations. Furthermore, Spencer and Hardimon are defending a view of races as biological and not merely scientific. As such, the kinds of explanatory value they secure must be those sought by biological sciences. And as I have argued, it is these values they fail to secure.

In the next section, I turn to *social* conceptions of race. I begin with accounts of the social construction of race and discuss their main features.

## 3 Social Constructionism about Race

On December 21, 1848, Ellen and William Craft embarked on one of the most famous and daring escapes from slavery in American history. The story of their escape is all the more remarkable because their flight occurred in proverbial broad daylight, while traveling first class by train and staying at the best hotels. Ellen Craft was three-quarters "European" in her ancestry (a *quadroon* in the classification system of the French slave code and *black* according to the prevailing American racial classification system). Her father was her mother's, and therefore her, owner. She was light-skinned and resembled her father and half-siblings. Chagrined that the young Ellen often passed as a member of the family, the matriarch of the family gave eleven-year-old Ellen as a wedding present for her daughter (and Ellen's half sister) Eliza. The newly married couple settled in Macon in 1837 with Ellen in tow.

William Craft was a skilled carpenter and cabinet maker in Macon. He had witnessed the destruction of his family at the auction block as his parents and siblings were separated by sales at different times to different owners. Ellen and William met in Macon and courted for many years, hesitant to marry on account of the terrible experiences they both bore as slaves. They eventually did marry and soon after hatched the plan for their escape (Craft 1860). William describes the genesis of their escape plan:

> Knowing that slaveholders have the privilege of taking their slaves to any part of the country they think proper, it occurred to me that, as my wife was nearly white, I might get her to disguise herself as an invalid gentleman, and assume to be my master, while I could attend as his slave, and that in this manner we might effect our escape. (Craft 1860, 16)

William carefully purchased the items they would need, using wages he earned working overtime as a cabinetmaker. The most sensitive items of clothing Ellen sewed herself and kept locked in a chest William had made for her. Once they were ready, they secured passes to be away for Christmas from their owners and took off. Ellen had her hair cut short and put her arm in a sling (the "invalid gentleman" disguise being necessary because neither Ellen nor William were literate). Although they were nearly caught during several legs of their journey, the Crafts arrived safely in Philadelphia, and to freedom, on Christmas Day 1848.

Two features of Craft's account are worth noting for our purposes. First, interspersed with the narrative of their escape, William Craft includes vignettes about the experiences of other enslaved black people to highlight the role of race in the legal and political regime of slave states. The right to buy and sell goods, legal standing in courts, the right to basic education or the obligation not to extend it, among myriad others, created a system of racial domination. As Craft notes, the law as written – although explicitly designed to enshrine white supremacy – does not fully capture the extent to which blacks were deprived of even minimal effective legal rights. In the antebellum south, to be black meant one is subject to the law while receiving no protection from it; to be white is to have the protection of the law and impunity in one's dealings with black and enslaved people.

The second notable feature of Craft's account is the dependence of racial classification on the social and political context particular to a given society. For instance, the status of Ellen Craft as a black woman, having no more or fewer legal privileges than any other black slave in Georgia is a specific aspect of the American racial system. Racial classification systems in the Caribbean and Latin America varied widely in how they racialized individuals based on ancestry, social class, immigration status, and other real or imagined character-istics (Telles and Paschel 2014). Whether Ellen was racialized as black or quadroon did not matter at all in the American South but would have mattered a great deal in Cuba or Haiti. The difference between these racial systems was the result of social and political considerations and not in the first instance a consequence of their differing understanding of human biology.

The Crafts' narrative, and others like it, are the kinds of illustrative cases used by proponents of viewing race as a mainly or entirely social phenomenon. It certainly does much to motivate the claim that social and historical consider-ations played a prominent role in the formation of ordinary or folk racial ideas. It lends itself to an influential and widely accepted approach to understanding phenomena like the Craft narrative that holds *race is socially constructed.*

Social constructionism about race[26] is a family of views that holds that racial groups are demarcated primarily on the basis of social factors (such as culture, institutions, and politics, among others).[27] Constructionism is a broad view, encompassing many distinct metaphysical views. These views can broadly be categorized as *political* and *cultural* constructionism.[28] Political and cultural constructionism agree on the origins of race as a social category but disagree on the present and future of race. On both accounts, race emerged as

---

[26] This view is sometimes called racial constructivism or social constructivism about race. I use these terms interchangeably.

[27] See Outlaw (1996); Mills (1998); Haslanger (2000, 2012), Glasgow et al.(2019); Mallon (2006).

[28] For an alternative taxonomy, see Mallon (2006, 534), who divides constructionism into *thin, interactive kind,* and *institutional* variants.

a consequence, and justification, of hierarchical power relations. However, for the cultural constructionist, race does not presently *depend* on these hierarchies to persist. The political history of race has a cultural afterlife that is strong enough to sustain racial identity even in the absence of racial inequality.

For political constructionists, on the other hand, race and hierarchy are inextricably linked. To see how, I next discuss two prominent political constructionist accounts from Charles Mills (1998) and Sally Haslanger (2000, 2012) and Glasgow et al. (2019).

## 3.1 Mills on Racial Constructivism

In an influential account, Charles Mills (1998) defends *racial constructivism*, "a view of race as both real and unreal, not 'realist' but still objectivist" (Mills 1998, 47). It is "unreal" in so far as the essentialist or biological assumptions of nineteenth century race science, which played a prominent role in shaping dominant conceptions of race, are false. Nevertheless, race has an "objective ontological status" due to the intersubjective judgment that underpins it. The fact that people conceive of themselves and others as "raced" grounds the social reality of race.

Mills (1998, 42) introduces a thought experiment to motivate the ontological status of race as both social and real. Mills (1998) asks us to imagine a society in which individuals are assigned a *quace* (Q1, Q2, Q3, etc.). This assignment is generated randomly by a computer and does not track any morphological or geological facts. Everyone's quace is registered in official documents such as state IDs, passports, naturalization papers, and so on. However, quace lacks any social significance beyond the mere fact that everyone has a quace. If anyone asked what one's quace was, one would merely report what was listed in official documents.

Mills (1998) notes that quacial membership lacks "ontological depth." There isn't a quace anyone "really" is in the society described by Mills. As Mills puts it, "'I am a Q1!' would have no metaphysical ring, no broader historical resonance to it, any more than our declaration of our passport number has any metaphysical ring or broader historical resonance to it" (Mills 1998, 42). Race, on the other hand, has deep social and metaphysical significance. If we picture Ellen Craft in her disguise as a white man and ask, what is she[29] *really*? We are drawing a sharp line between appearance and reality. We are claiming that her race is more than skin-deep. It is worth noting that the inquiry does not arise because her racial identity is ambiguous. Although there aren't any uniform,

---

[29] In using female pronouns, I am bracketing an equally interesting set of questions in relation to gender.

universally applied norms of racial classification in any society, what draws interest in this case is precisely that there is a definite answer one can give depending on just which norms one appeals to (e.g., one drop rule). And this, Mills argues, is the result of two major divergences between race (in our world) and quace. First, race classification is (generally) based on identifiable morphological features. Second, race, at least in most modern societies, is a vertical system. That is, races are hierarchically placed along several dimensions (social, political, economic, etc.).

The comparison of quace and race is meant to highlight a core thesis of constructivist accounts of race, what I'll call the *contingency thesis*. The contingency thesis holds that the racial categories and their hierarchical position are contingent on social and historical facts. The racial categories could have been demarcated differently than they were, or race as it came to be understood could have failed to arise. One line of evidence for the contingency thesis is the diversity of racial classification systems in the actual world. Since the number, type, and boundary of racial categories vary even among societies that are not isolated from one another, it is not a leap to suppose that dramatically different racial classification schemes could have dominated given sufficiently different social conditions. As Malik (1996) and Smith (2015) show, the racial essentialism that came to dominate in the nineteenth century had contested origins and could have failed to launch if it were not met with the historical conditions that facilitated its prominence. Consequently, for racial constructivists, it is from *social* facts that race draws its metaphysical import. Race is not part of the natural order of things. We do not discover races in the way scientists once discovered, for instance, the circulation of the blood or the temperature at which copper is a superconductor. Rather, race is made and maintained by the social power it has.

## 3.2 Haslanger on the Hierarchical Foundations of Race

Sally Haslanger (2000, 2012) and Glasgow et al. (2019) defend a critical and anti-racist approach to the metaphysics of race. Haslanger's project is not merely descriptive, attempting to capture the race concept with a high degree of accuracy. Rather, a *critical* metaphysical analysis should allow us to achieve the goals of social justice such as combating racism. Glasgow et al. (2019) argues that in determining what race is "the goal is to provide an interpretation of what has plausibly been at issue (though not always clearly at issue) "all along," as evidenced not only by what we say, but what we do, such as the practices we engage in, the laws we pass, and social scientific explanations of these" (Glasgow et al. 2019, 16). An answer to the question "what is race?"

ought to illuminate a host of social and political phenomena that extend beyond what might initially appear to be the narrow theoretical confines of metaphysics. A critical theorist wants an account of race that makes sense of the role of race in our social lives and how to upend the injustices in which it is enmeshed.

Haslanger's analysis proceeds from the conclusion that there are no human biological groups that correspond to the essentialist or biologically realist conceptions of race. Rather, races are social categories. They are, nonetheless, no less real for it. While Haslanger rejects analyses of race as biological, this is not cause to jettison race talk altogether. A critical theorist still seeks to use race to limn the social realities created by historical and ongoing sociopolitical practices. Race helps explain inequalities and deprivations that are differentially distributed across a society like the United States. The best way to achieve these analytic and normative aims is with a social constructionist approach.

On Haslanger's critical account, race is embedded within social hierarchies. These social hierarchies are stratified on the basis of real or imagined physical features such as skin color, eye shape, hair texture, and so on that are taken to indicate ancestry and geographic origin. Racialization is the process of assigning evaluative meaning to these real or imagined physical features. Haslanger (2000) thus provides the following account:

> A group is racialized iff$_{df}$ its members are socially positioned as subordinate or privileged along some dimension (economic, political, legal, social, etc.), and the group is "marked" as a target for this treatment by observed or imagined bodily features presumed to be evidence of ancestral links to a certain geographical region. (Haslanger 2000, 44)

This account has many explanatory virtues. For one, it helps us see that the different racial classifications in different societies do not undermine the utility of a race concept. What unifies race across these different contexts is that race serves the same sociopolitical role. Namely, racialization creates racial categories and places individuals in those categories based on real or imagined physical "markers" such as skin color or eye form. The racial categories might vary from one society to the next. But their hierarchical role remains.

Take for instance the differences between the slave codes in Virginia and French Saint-Domingo in the eighteenth century. The latter had a category, mulatto, for individuals of "mixed" white and black ancestry. Whereas colonial Virginia had a rule of hypodescent, where the "mixed" offspring were assigned the race of the subordinate parent. This meant in practice that the child of a white slaver and his black slave was racialized as black. Virginia planters were not unfamiliar with the mulatto concept. However, mulatto came to have a far more distinct and socially consequential status in the French colonies along with maroon, octoroon, and other categories of "mixed" racial ancestry. These individuals made up a large share of the free population, could marry into white families, and some even owned slaves.

The explanation for the divergence was in part due to the demographic composition of these societies. Because of the difficulty of living in the French Caribbean posed by diseases such as yellow fever, there was relatively very little migration from France to the Caribbean colonies. As a result, the white population of Saint-Domingo was extremely small at about forty thousand in the late eighteenth century (Hunt 2006, 9). This engendered the need to expand the free population in order to stabilize the social order, one constituted by extraordinarily harsh and deadly living and working conditions for the enslaved population. American colonies and states of the antebellum US, on the other hand, did not have such a lopsided population structure between free whites and enslaved blacks. The relatively large white population meant that managing the enslaved population was manageable even if the social order excluded people of any black ancestry from an intermediate position within the social hierarchy. The economic value of, say, Ellen Craft as a slave exceeded any social value from creating a more stable sociopolitical order through the expansion of a group of free people racialized in an intermediate node between white and black. In those social circumstances, it is more provident for the planter class to racialize Ellen into the same category as William or any other enslaved persons. We see here, therefore, a demonstration of the real basis for racial classification, namely, the sociopolitical forces that prevail in society. And transforming those forces – through egalitarian political action for instance – will have the result of knocking out the base of race.

## 3.3 Racial Equality

One implication of political constructionist accounts such as Haslanger's (2000, 2012) and Glasgow et al.'s (2019) characterization of race is that racial equality is not a coherent outcome of justice. Racialization is always a process that places races in a social hierarchy. Achieving social justice would have the result of robbing social significance from the real or imagined physical features on which racialization depends. An America in which black people enjoy the same opportunities – in education, health care, employment, and housing, among others – on the same terms as white people, and do not disproportionately occupy disadvantaged social roles such as the *ghetto poor*[30] or higher rates of incarceration, is one in which the defining (hierarchical) boundary between white and black would collapse.

---

[30] See Shelby (2016) for a discussion of the origins and persistence of racialized urban ghettos.

How could this be so? If dark-skinned people with kinky hair come from Africa, and light-skinned people with smooth hair come from Europe, these visible physical features could plausibly serve as a stable and robust basis for racial categories even if membership in these categories does not entail patterns of subordination. However, there is reason to think this is not as implausible as it seems. One of the remarkable facts of the history of racialization is just how malleable and fluid racial categories have been. The varied practices of racialization in non-US contexts only help to illustrate this point. The physical features that seem an obvious and robust basis for the persistence of racial categories are missing in some cases of racialization. In other instances, racialization occurs on the basis of imagined physical differences or seemingly irrelevant facts such as social class. As Telles and Paschel (2014) note in their study of racialization in Latin America, "... the relation between color and status with racial identification and the use of mixed-race categories – reflects the country's distinct sets of historical and contemporary inducements" (Telles and Paschel 2014, 867). In societies where status and racial identification are intimately linked, equality would undermine continued differential racialization. Racialization knits together real or imagined physical features and social facts that do not have to coincide. But it knits them in iron. This does not mean that the effects of racialization are insurmountable. Nonetheless, undoing them involves a revolutionary reconfiguring of society in much of the world where race has taken on a paramount role in social life.

## 3.4 Cultural Constructionism

It is safe to say that on the political constructionist accounts we have so far discussed the tale of race is a tale of woe. Oppression, subordination, and hierarchy are the bases of the social reality of race. However, social construction need not take a wholly negative view of the consequences of social construction of race. Chike Jeffers (2013) and Glasgow et al. (2019) defend a *cultural constructionist* account of race which he contrasts with *political constructionism*. While both are species of social construction, Glasgow et al. (2019) argues that races are both politically and culturally constructed (Glasgow et al. 2019, 55). Races are politically constructed broadly in the way outlined by the accounts of philosophers such as Mills (1998) and Haslanger (2000, 2012). That is, races are created and maintained primarily through differential power relations between racialized groups. Glasgow et al. (2019) adds that a relatively neglected aspect of social construction is that racialization has a cultural component. Outlaw (1996) highlighted culture as fundamental to the social construction of race. Glasgow et al. (2019) advances this approach in opposition to views like Haslanger's that hold that in the absence of differential power relations and hierarchies, races would lose the basis of their social reality.

Political and cultural constructionism agree on the nature of the *origins* of race. On both accounts, race is the product of sociohistorical factors where groups marked by (real or imagined) physical features are placed in a social hierarchy. Where the two accounts diverge is on the question of what *presently* maintains the continued social reality of race. For political constructionists, differential power relations are fundamental to the present reality of race. For cultural constructionists, race would survive the end of racism. That is, the different ways of life that accompany the process of racialization would persist and therefore maintain the reality of race. In a world without racial hierarchy, Glasgow et al. (2019) argues, race would entirely be grounded in culture. As such, culture is as fundamental to race as politics.

There are two claims that should be disambiguated. The first claim is that races, as a result of their unique history and social circumstances, come to have distinctive cultures. These cultures are valuable even if the context in which they were engendered is unjust. A second claim is that a group is racial in *virtue of* its distinctive culture, to be a racial group is to have a *distinctive way of life*. It is the latter, stronger, claim that is culturally constructionist about race. Glasgow et al. (2019) rejects the essentialist thesis that different races belong to different civilizations. Nonetheless, he argues, it is still the case that people come to have pride in their culture *qua* race. For instance, a black American child can feel pride in the achievements of ancient African civilization even if he may not be connected to them through close ancestry. Movements such as "Black is Beautiful" answer to a real feeling among black individuals that their physical features, markers of inferiority in racist societies, are intrinsically valuable and aesthetically pleasing. These facts of "racial consciousness" can ground the practices that are sufficient to continue sustaining the social reality of race.

Jeffers' cultural constructionism makes a valuable contribution to thinking about social race. Social race is not just political, it is also cultural. Moreover, the experience of racialization is not entirely negative. Racial solidarity and cultural forms of belonging are engendered by the act of seeing oneself as part of a racial group. However, the cultural constructionist account has flaws. Crucially, "cultures" are too fluid, amorphous, and numerous to do the work of grounding race. In an infamous 1988 New York Times Magazine interview with James Atlas, the American writer Saul Bellow once asked "who is the Tolstoy of the Zulus, the Proust of the Papuans? I'd be glad to read him" (Atlas 1988). To which question the journalist Raph Wiley much later answered, and in my view perfectly so, "Tolstoy is the Tolstoy of the Zulus – unless you find a profit in fencing off universal properties of mankind into exclusive tribal ownership" (Wiley 1996). In a world rid of racism, I can hardly see how Wiley's view would not be widely shared. And in that world, a black child may find herself as proud of a Bernini as she is of the Benin Bronzes. Such a world will lack (racialized) cultural barriers that can maintain the social reality of race.

## 3.5 Social Construction Instead of What?

The title of Ian Hacking's (1999) influential book on social construction asked, "*The Social Construction of What?*" It is even more instructive to ask social construction *instead of what?* For Hacking (1999), constructionist accounts of any X are necessarily revisionist. The purpose of identifying some X as socially constructed is to debunk an essentialist conception. That is, the claim that X is socially constructed is "used to undermine the idea that X is essential, even that X has an 'essence'" (Hacking 1999, 16). There would be no point to the use of "social construction" if what is claimed as constructed wasn't commonly taken to be inevitable or essential, part of the furniture of the universe (as such, things like money and laws are not on Hacking's account socially constructed in so far as they are widely understood to be social creations that can be altered through social processes). For instance, there is no social constructionism about money because it is common knowledge that money is the result of sociopolitical and economic human activities. Furthermore, social constructionists often urge that "X is quite bad as it is" and "we would be much better off if X were done away with, or at least radically transformed" (Hacking 1999, 6). Constructionist views therefore frequently come as part of a package that includes normative commitments.

Haslanger (2012) agrees with Hacking (1999) that "the discourse of social construction functions differently in different contexts … " (2012, 113). Some social constructionists defend their view as an analysis of race that rescues the concept from a biological conception and instead emphasizes the social, (and/or) cultural, factors that shape the formation and use of racial categories (cf. Sundstrom 2002). To view race as socially constructed is to hold that race does not exist independently of historically contingent social practices. By emphasizing the social and historical origins of race, social constructionists aim to expose the ways in which race is used to perpetuate social inequality and oppression. In any case, a view can hardly be called social constructionist unless it disclaims essentialism. What set of conditions get defined as essentialist is of course a matter of dispute. Since race essentialism has fallen out of favor even among those who maintain a commitment to a biological conception of race, the question arises as to how biological racial realism and social constructionism are related. That is, is social construction a view one must hold *instead of* a biological conception of race? For many proponents of both social construction and biological racial realism, the answer is no (Kitcher 2007; Hardimon 2017a; Glasgow et al. 2019; Hochman 2022).

The relationship between social construction and biological racial realism is more complicated than the one between constructionism and essentialism. Biological racial realism rejects those aspects of essentialism that social constructionists find objectionable, including holding that races are immutable or have rigid boundaries. Yet it still captures what might be objectionable from a social constructivist point of view. Namely, biological racial realism holds that race has independence from human actions and intentions. To claim race is a biological category is to hold that races *are* part of the nature of things. Race may be socially contingent, but it is not biologically contingent. At least some of our race concepts carve (human) nature at its joints.

However, certain features of the constructionist view suggest that constructionism about race is not necessarily committed to biological anti-realism. Advocates of a biological conception of race such as Kitcher (2007, 2012), Spencer (2014, 2018), and Glasgow et al. (2019) maintain the compatibility of biological race and racial constructivism.[31] For instance, as discussed in Section 2.2, Kitcher argues that there are conditions in which "races are both biologically real and socially constructed" and that there is no contradiction between the two positions (Kitcher 2007, 298). Spencer defends an account where the racial categories set out by the 1997 OMB racial classification scheme, a case of a social institution engaged in racialization par excellence, are also biologically meaningful. Spencer's argument is that at least *some* of our conceptions of race, the OMB scheme as he defends it, are biological. As such there is no opposition between his biological account and constructivism about race.

Hochman (2022) argues that the compatibility of social construction with social realist, biological realist, and even anti-realist accounts of race renders the constructivist approach moot. He writes "if 'social constructionism' can mean almost anything, then – without further clarification – it means almost nothing. Or rather, we might say that it means whatever the reader believes it to mean, which could be any number of things" (Hochman 2022, 48). Regardless of whether racial constructivism fails to exclude alternative metaphysical pictures, for many constructivists, it is not merely a project for achieving descriptive accuracy about race. Rather, constructivism is partly a project with normative aims (e.g., achieving social justice) (Haslanger 2000; Mallon 2006). As such, the metaphysical account partly depends on these normative

---

[31] See also Andreasen (2005) and Hardimon (2017a).

aims. If the race concept is to help us in our normative endeavor of bringing about justice, or undoing historical injustice, one way it can do so is by aiding our understanding of social reality. Race, perhaps, allows us to limn the causal structure of our social world. It enables us to make predictions and identifies sites of intervention for our political ameliorative work.

In the next section, I turn to the putative role of social race in (social) science.

## 3.6 Race and Social Structural Explanation

Let's take the explanation of how I ended up in London. Suppose I were to take a train down to London from Leeds.[32] One explanation could cite the speed at which my body was accelerating toward London, including details about what happened as I stood up to walk around or change seats, among other physical facts specific to my body. Another explanation could cite the fact that there was a train from Leeds to London and that I was on it. The latter explanation strikes us as being more valuable. It is the train that travels from Leeds to London. I am just along for the ride. This type of explanation, where we explain the behavior of an entity by explaining the behavior of a larger entity of which it is a part, is ubiquitous in the sciences.

Haslanger (2016) argues that what makes the explanation of the latter type more valuable is that they are, among other things, *stable*. The fact that I end up in London (the explanandum-phenomenon) is invariant across a range of interventions: whether I speed up or slow down on my way from Leeds, whether I arrive late or on time, and so on. The causal constraints on the realization of the explanandum are those of the containing entity. That is, whether or not I end up in London depends on the causal constraints and capacities of the train.

This, then, is a structural explanation. We explain the behavior of an individual part by explaining the behavior of the containing structure. Haslanger (2016) provides a characterization of structures where "structures, broadly understood, are complex entities with parts whose behavior is constrained by their relation to other parts" (Haslanger 2016, 118). Structures are not mere aggregates. Unlike aggregates, the interaction between the parts of structures constrains their activity. Furthermore, it is not just physical objects that constitute structures. *Social* structures play a central explanatory role in the social sciences. Haslanger writes, "Structures are important to explanation because they constrain behavior of individual things insofar as they occupy nodes in the structure. The structure does not simply provide background conditions for the events in question [.], for it is the workings of the structure that are sometimes the proper object explanation[...]" (Haslanger 2016, 121)

---

[32] This adapts a similar illustrative case from Haslanger (2016).

To see how, let's take up the case of the Crafts' flight from slavery again. Explanandum: Why does Ellen dress like a man during their escape?

We can provide an explanation in terms of her psychological states and individual choices. Let's call this an *Individual Explanation*. For instance, we can cite Ellen's beliefs, goals, and desires to explain her choice to dress like a man. However, the *Individual Explanation* fails to capture explanatorily deep facts that strike us as relevant. To capture these facts, we will need to appeal to social structures. The Crafts lived in a racially stratified slave society. It was also a patriarchal society. As such, Ellen and William Craft were embedded as "nodes" within a hierarchical structure constituted by specific race and gender relations. Haslanger (2016) writes "my actions are my own, triggered by my thoughts, desires, goals. However, the resources I rely on and the meaning of my action are not mine alone but depend on the structure I'm part of. Illumination of these structures is important for explaining human action" (128). For a white woman to travel unaccompanied with her male slave would be as incongruous as seeing a black couple purchase a first-class train ticket. Crafts' options for an escape that made use of their particular resources and attributes – Ellen's light skin tone, William's carpentry, their standing with their enslavers, and so on – were constrained by the patriarchal and racialized social structures they sought to flee in plain sight.

As Haslanger (2016) notes, structural constraints make it so that only some options are genuine possibilities (124). An explanation of why Ellen dressed as a man who does not cite these social structural facts would be worse than one that does. The social structural explanation illuminates the full range of normatively relevant facts. For instance, the intersection between gender and race relations represented by the fact that a white woman would not travel alone with her black slave is explanatorily related to the justifications for lynchings of black men a century later. Furthermore, the social structural explanation itself explains the individual psychological states and individual choices that constitute an alternative explanans. Ellen believes she must dress as a man as a result of the social practices and relations in which she was brought up. "The focus on structural constraints," then, "provides resources for capturing significant regularities: those whose choices are similarly constrained will tend to act in similar ways, even if their personal histories, psychologies, and attitudes differ" (124).

What kinds of constraints are structural constraints? Ross (2023) proposes that at least some of these social structures impose causal constraints. She defends an interventionist account of how social structures can be causal and explanatory. On the interventionist framework, "to say that X is a cause of Y means that an intervention that changes the values of X, in some background conditions B, will produce changes in the values of Y" (Ross 2023, 8). The intervention need not be actually possible. However, much of social science investigates social structures by means of experimental manipulation or by using "natural experiments" in which exogenous factors have changed the experimental variable. Social scientists exploit differences in variables of interest – differential roll out of new policies, disparate impact of economic shocks in different locales, and so on – to identify causal-explanatory factors. To claim that, for instance, school-based nutrition improves learning, is to hold that intervening on school-based nutrition directly changes learning outcomes.

The explanatory challenge of appealing to social structures arises because structures are composed of agents who then make choices we seek to explain by appealing to those structures. Furthermore, structural explanations seem to involve a seemingly mysterious and controversial type of causation, namely, top-down causation. A natural suggestion is that agents and the social structures they inhabit are interdependent. Social structures (causally) constrain agents and agents in turn constitute social structures (that is, social structures depend on agents for their existence). Ross (2023) argues that "in social structural explanations, structure and individual agency are interacting causes with respect to some effect of interest. This framework captures that structure and agency are different properties, that they take on different values, and that they depend on each other in producing outcomes" (Ross 2023, 9).

The value of this approach lies in that it accounts for how social structures can be more explanatory, or provide more valuable explanations, than individual agency. For Ross (2023), "[structural] causal constraints have additional features that are not present in standard, run-of-the-mill causes. These constraints can interact with other causal factors and they exert influence on them – they guide, limit, and shape the outcomes produced by other causes" (Ross 2023, 6). The additional features of structural causal constraints are that they (1) limit the values of the explanatory target of interest, (2) are often conceived of as separate from or external to the process they limit, (3) are considered relatively fixed compared to other explanatory factors, and (4) structure or guide the explanandum outcome, as opposed to triggering it (Ross 2023, 10–11).

What these features together entail is that social structural explanations secure dimensions of explanatory value such as stability and proportionality. As such, explanations that cite the social role of race as a structuring phenomenon will have this value. By determining what options are available to agents in the first place, social structures carve the explanatory space to a greater degree than individual choices. In the example of the Crafts, we see agents who are severely limited in the kinds of choices available to them by the social structure of which they are a part. Although they partly compose this social structure, they do not constrain it. Social structures are relatively fixed and change over long timescales (Ross 2023, 10). Agents are for the most part limited to selection among choices that social structures make available. Furthermore, we can see that *social race* is an explanatory fecund category in the social sciences (Mallon 2018). Unlike in the case of (minimalist) biological races, the racial level is the appropriate grain for securing dimensions of explanatory value such as depth and specific when explaining social phenomena. The conception of race as a social kind, therefore, is able to secure race as a genuine kind in a way minimalist biological racial realism cannot.[33] If that is the case, social race is an indispensable element of our explanation of a whole host of phenomena in sociology, economics, and political science.

In the final section, I turn to anti-realist theories of race.

## 4 Anti-realism about Race

In 1589, ten-year old Jane Throckmorton, who had been ill with "violent sneezing and grotesque seizures," accused seventy-six-year old Alice Samuel, who was at the time visiting the Throckmortons at their family home, of witchcraft (DeWindt 1995, 427 f). This incident set off a chain of events culminating in the trial, conviction, and execution of Alice Samuel and members of her family for witchcraft in 1612. The "Warboys Witches" as they came to be known, were poor tenants of Robert Throckmorton, Jane's father and one of the most prominent men of Elizabethan England. Jane's accusation was bolstered by doctors from Cambridge who suggested her symptoms were the result of magic.

The ordinary concept of *witch*, as it developed in the Europe and colonial America of the late medieval and early modern periods (roughly 1450–1750 CE), referred to an individual, usually but not always a woman, who has supernatural powers either innately or through dealings with malign spirits and powers, principally the devil. Underpinning the popular witchcraft beliefs of these societies was a broader constellation of beliefs including "in occult, or hidden, forces and ethereal conscious entities that influence the visible material world; an array of words, rituals, and objects employed to harness or defend against them; a set of practitioners who specialized in interacting with them; and a conviction that some people utilized them to injure others" (Bever 2013, 51). Witchcraft beliefs fit into the dominant Christian cosmology of the time, which included belief in supernatural

---

[33] For an opposing view, see Khalifa and Lauer (2021), who argue social race does not contribute to the epistemic success of social sciences. Similarly, Singh and Wodak (2024) argue that race need not figure into our explanations of, for instance, racial discrimination. Appeal to racial attitudes alone is sufficient.

entities such as angels and demons and religious rituals surrounding life cycle (birth, marriage, death, etc.) and natural cycle events.

Witchcraft beliefs were not identical in the complex and diverse societies of Europe and colonial America. In continental Europe (particularly German-speaking societies) and Scotland, witches were taken to engage in occult rituals called Satan's Sabbath. In England, witches were not associated with Satan's Sabbath. Rather *maleficium*, which are calamities including illness, and death of humans and cattle, were the principal mark of witchcraft. Witches were typically thought to be identifiable by certain marks on their bodies where the Devil is said to have touched or that they used to feed their demonic familiars. Continental Europe and the common law jurisdictions of England and colonial America also had differing evidentiary standards for conviction for witchcraft and the severity of the sentence. Nonetheless, there was a recognizable pattern of who was accused of witchcraft across these societies. They were usually made against elderly women of lower status, particularly those with reputations for being "quarrelsome or disreputable" (Bever 2013, 53). An accusation of witchcraft against a person also cast suspicion on relatives, since it was widely believed magical powers were hereditary. In Scotland alone, an estimated 4,000 witches were accused and perhaps 2,500 were executed (Goodare 2013, 300).

By the close of the early modern period belief in witchcraft began to wane. In 1735, a new witchcraft act was passed by the British parliament. Unlike in previous legislation, the 1735 act criminalized *the pretense* of having supernatural powers in order to sell magical items and services. What were once a series of laws enacted to protect people from dark occult forces were replaced by a law meant to protect consumers from fraud. As Bever writes, "by the nineteenth century, it had become possible to argue that witches had never really existed, that even self-styled ones were the product, rather than the source, of demonology" (Bever 2013, 68). As such, we (modern people) have ceased to believe in witches. Which is to say that we do not believe there are people who, through a pact with demonic forces, have supernatural powers which they chiefly use to harm others. We do not appeal to witches or witchcraft to explain any phenomena, even those that seem hard to explain by naturalistic means. Our criminal justice system does not recognize witchcraft as a crime, nor does anyone have legal standing to accuse another of witchcraft practices. Encouragingly, a concept with such a fraught and deadly historical legacy is now mostly the subject of children's storytelling and adult amusement.

*Racial anti-realism*[34] is a view that holds that the concept of race fails to pick out anything real in the world. This metaphysical view is distinct but related to

---

[34] In the literature this view is sometimes called *racial skepticism* (Mallon 2006).

the normative view called *racial eliminativism*, which holds that, given races are not real, we ought to discard the use of race.[35] I began the section on racial anti-realism with a digression on witchcraft for two reasons. First, many racial anti-realists draw an analogy between the race and witch concepts (Appiah 1996, 2007; Glasgow 2009; Blum 2010; Fields and Fields 2012; Hochman 2017; Wodak 2022). And with good reason, there are striking parallels between the ordinary concepts of witch and race. Both concepts involve widely shared but occasionally divergent sets of associated beliefs. Unlike other concepts discarded on the scrapheap of ontology, such as "phlogiston" and "vitalism," they are sociopolitically consequential in societies that deploy them. And, for the racial anti-realist, both race and witch point to something that does not exist.[36]

The witch analogy also holds another promise for the racial anti-realist. Race remains a powerful and pervasive presence in many contemporary societies. Indeed, it seems to be strengthening, rather than waning, in salience in places like the United States. In the preface and acknowledgments to her book *Race and Mixed Race*, Naomi Zack presents an illuminating personal account of the changes in the role of race in her lifetime. She writes "during my student years, race was not an issue for me: I did not have to identify myself racially on any forms, and I do not remember any official person in the New York City public school system, in college, or in graduate school asking me what race I was" (Zack 1993, xi). This state of affairs, Zack writes, was much changed in the decades that followed as exemplified by the increased attention to race in academia after 1970 (Zack 1993, xii).

It is difficult to imagine what it means to claim races are not real or that the racial discourse ought to be eliminated. However, as briefly noted in this section's opening, the witch concept underwent a remarkable historical development, from a widely believed concept with life-and-death consequences for tens of thousands of people across Europe and colonial America, to a discredited notion with scarcely any contemporary relevance beyond historical or cultural interest. These changes allow us to see how, if the anti-realist is right, a concept such as race (which purports to capture something that does not exist) comes to have the significance that it does. As Appiah (1996, 38) writes, " . . . we may need to understand talk of 'witchcraft' to understand how people respond cognitively and how they act in

---

[35] Wodak (2022) argues that rather than being about eliminating race from our vocabulary, eliminativism should be about how we ought to *use* race terms.

[36] I am bracketing here the non-trivial issue raised by people who self-identify as "witches" because they practice the New Age religion of Wicca. In this case it seems natural to say that the same term, "witch," is being used for two different concepts (Glasgow 2009, 7).

a culture that has a concept of witchcraft, whether or not we think there are, in fact, any witches."

Kwame Anthony Appiah (1996) argues that there is no set of coherent beliefs associated with race. Nor is there a stable referent for the concept. This is due to the fact that "current ways of talking about race are the residue, the detritus, so to speak, of earlier ways of thinking about race; so that it turns out to be easiest to understand contemporary talk about "race" as the pale reflection of a more full-blooded race discourse that flourished in the last century" (Appiah 1996, 38). As we have seen in previous sections, the development of racial ideas was highly contingent and contested. Across societies and within them, a host of muddled and sometimes contradictory beliefs accreted to "folk" race thinking. There is therefore nothing real that can answer to the term race.

Consider also Barbara and Karen Fields' (2012) groundbreaking book *Racecraft*, whose title is a direct reference to witchcraft. Fields and Fields (2012) defend racial anti-realism that grounds race in the ideological role it played (and plays) in Western societies. Fields and Fields (2012) argue that just as witchcraft beliefs draw their power from the ideological, social, and political role played by, among other things, witch hunts, in order to understand race we must understand the sociopolitical context in which race-ing is practiced. The ideological conception of race is the transformation of sociopolitical choices into natural and inevitable categories. For instance, writing about skin color – the quintessential racial trait – Fields (1982) notes:

> Ideas about color, like ideas about anything else derive their importance, indeed their very definition, from their context. They can no more be the unmediated reflex of psychic impressions than can any other ideas. It is their ideological context that tells people which details to notice, which to ignore, and which to take for granted in translating the world around them into ideas about the world. (Fields 1982, 146)

The rules for this "translation" vary from one society to another, even in the same polities. Nevertheless, members of a society are able to instantly apply the rules. The rules depend on specific social contexts, and the contexts in turn are shaped by dominant sociopolitical actors. Fields and Fields (2012) argue that the ideological use of race is in creating and perpetuating social inequalities that benefit those placed in the privileged position of these racial hierarchies (Fields and Fields 2012). The witch analogy allows us to imagine a post*race* world. Just as a European society in the grips of a witch hunt can scarcely imagine a world where witchcraft is largely the stuff of children's entertainment. So too is our imagination of a postrace world potentially limited by the pervasiveness of race.

Of course, many of the features of the analogy between the race and witch concepts are agreeable to racial constructivism. On both racial anti-realist and constructivist accounts, the dominant ordinary conceptions of race embed false naturalistic or biological premises. Consequently, there is nothing in nature to which the ordinary concepts of race and witch refer. However, as discussed in Section 2, although racial constructivists deny the reality of ordinary races, they argue race is still real in virtue of the social system in which people are *raced*. Anti-realists on the other hand, argue that the appropriate response to the fact that nothing in the world matches up with the ordinary concept of race is to conclude there are no such things as races (Zack 1993; Appiah 1996). The witch analogy is here further illuminating. Once we accept the nonexistence of witches, we begin to talk of *people accused of being* witches or people *claiming to be* witches, and so on, a procedure anti-realists argue ought to hold for race as well.

## 4.1 Mismatch Objection

The mismatch objection[37] is a prominent argument against various metaphysical proposals concerning race that exploits the distinction between how race is *ordinarily* understood and the revisionist accounts many philosophers defend (see Appiah 1996; Glasgow 2003, 2009; Andreasen 2005; Mallon 2006; Zack 2014). Racial anti-realism holds there are no races because the ordinary or folk concepts of race refer to entities that do not exist. This is partly because there are conceptual constraints to which groupings of humans can be *racial*. Among the conceptual constraints on what constitutes ordinary races is the fact that races are "relatively large groups of people who are distinguished from other groups of people by having certain visible biological traits (such as skin colors) to a disproportionate extent" (Glasgow et al. 2019, 117). First, races are relatively large groups of people that divide humanity into a handful of groups. From Blumenbach to the United States Office of Management and Budget, $R = 5$ has been a common and influential division of humans into races. Let's call this the *size constraint*. Of course, as we have seen in previous discussions, racial categories are not identical across time and different cultures. Racialization can increase or decrease in granularity depending on factors specific to a society. Nevertheless, as we have already seen it would violate the conceptual constraint of ordinary race to hold, for instance, that there are hundreds of human races.

Second, races are distinguished from one another by morphology. Let's call this the *visibility constraint*. This is not to claim that every individual is easily

---

[37] First so named by Mallon (2006).

identifiable as a member of a particular race. As in the case of Ellen Craft, it is possible for someone to "pass" as another race than the one to which they are ordinarily taken to belong. Rather, racial *groups* need to be distinguishable from other racial *groups* on the basis of visible biological traits such as skin color and eye shape. To motivate this condition, Glasgow (2009) asks us to imagine a scenario in which every human spontaneously begins to look roughly like the Dalai Lama. The thought is that intuitively a world of uniform physical appearance among humans is one that is devoid of human races (Glasgow 2009, 34). It may be ambiguous on the basis of visible traits to which racial group an individual belongs. But it seems conceptually befuddled to claim two groupings of humans that are physically indistinguishable from each other are different races. Armed with these two points, let us see how anti-realists use them to debunk both the biological and social reality of race.

The mismatch objection is that many revisionist philosophical proposals for racial groupings fail to comport with the ordinary concept of race. They fail either on the size or the visibility constraints, or both. Among the naturalistic proposals, mismatches arise because biologically significant groupings of humans are either coarser-grained, encompassing what are traditionally taken to be multiple different races, or are much finer-grained, smaller local ancestry groups and populations, than racial categories. For revisionist accounts drawing on biology, such as populational proposals that hold that races are isolated breeding populations (Andreasen 1998, 2000, 2004; Kitcher 1999, 2007), the objection is that "racial terms are applied to individuals in a way that does not map onto how science applies breeding population terms to individuals" (Glasgow 2009, 95).[38] Therefore, there is no biological category that is *racial*. Biology may subdivide humans, but it does not subdivide them into races.

## 4.2 Why Not Social Race?

Racial anti-realists reject not only the biological but also the *social* reality of races (Fields 1982; Fields and Fields 2012; Zack 1993, 2014; Appiah 1996; Blum 2002, 2010; Glasgow 2009). Social constructionism about race is open to a version of the mismatch objection. Constructionists and anti-realists share a crucial premise; the racial demarcating line is biologically arbitrary. It has no biological significance. Anti-realists go further and deny that *racialization* produces races even of a social kind. Anti-realist views grant that *racialization*, the practice of racial demarcation and differential treatment, is real. However, unlike constructionists, anti-realists deny that the resulting racialized groups are

---

[38] See Section 2.2 for a more detailed discussion.

races. Glasgow et al. (2019) argues that racialized groups and social races differ in key respects.

The first difference hinges on the *mind-dependence* of racialized groups. Racialized groups depend entirely on recognition in order to exist. Suppose we were to wake up one day, for instance, and forget all about our racial categories, then there would be no racialized groups. According to racial antirealists, in the state of amnesia about our practice of racial classification "races" would cease to exist because they depend on our social practice of racialization. Ordinary race, on the other hand, invokes a robust racial demarcation line that is invariant across a range of racialization practices. On the ordinary conception, races did not come to exist in the eighteenth century any more than the flower *Scilla italica* came to exist when Linnaeus first named and recorded it in his *Systema Naturae*. A statement such as "the origin of the black race is intimately tied up with the history of slavery and colonialism" is intuitively intelligible as a claim about when these racial classifications were made. However, the claim that the race *itself* emerged mere centuries ago is strikingly revisionary as an account of race. Revision is precisely what many racial constructivists propose. Racial anti-realists, however, deny that such a revision – if it severs the conceptual connection between race and biophysical difference – would result in the same concept (Zack 1993). Such a revised account, anti-realists argue, would no longer be an account of race as ordinarily understood.

The challenge to social race arises because racial constructionists take race to depend on contingent sociopolitical factors. The ordinary race concept, anti-realists argue, takes race to be more robust. As Glasgow et al. (2019) observes, "For all constructionists, if the relevant social facts, the ones that they think create race, are not in place, then race would disappear. This exposes all versions of constructionism to the different features problem: on the ordinary concept of race, race persists even when the social facts change" (Glasgow et al. 2019, 131). Whether is inequality, oppression, culture, or the act of racialization itself, constructionism holds that race depends on some social factor the disappearance of which would eliminate race. However, anti-realists contend, intuitively we can imagine a world of racial equality, or one where everyone has the same culture yet there are different racial groups, and so on. There is then a mismatch between the feature racial constructionism takes to be constitutive of race and the ordinary race concept. Consequently, the groups racialization produces cannot be the same groups referred to by *race*.

To conclude, anti-realist views of race deny that race has any reality whatsoever. Although the social practices that uphold race might be deeply entrenched and their consequences far-reaching, race would no more survive their transformation than the belief that certain scars mark a woman out as a servant of the devil. Eliminativists further argue that we can, and ought to, remove race from our common language or use it much the same way we use "witch."

## 5 Conclusion

What is race? It is not, as nearly all now agree, an essential and immutable division of humanity. Nonetheless, biological racial realists argue that it remains a biologically meaningful structure to human diversity. Such realists defend revisionist (Andreasen 2000; Pigliucci and Kaplan 2003; Kitcher 2007) or minimalist realism about race (Hardimon 2017a; Glasgow et al. 2019). Revisionists hold that we can subdivide humans into meaningful biological subgroups, but these will have little to no relation to the folk or ordinary concept of race. Minimalists argue that there are ordinary conceptions of race that are nonetheless biologically genuine. The view is minimalist because it does not claim that minimalist races explain a wide range of phenomena in biology, although it is possible that they do so. However, I have argued that minimalist races are an explanatorily stunted entity without the grounding in robust explanatory relations that may justify their status as a genuine kind or entity. Local populations and ancestry groups are frequently more explanatorily robust than the coarser-grained racial categories.

Social constructionist views of race contest essentialist race notions, and most take themselves to reject that race is a biological kind or entity. Constructivists characterize race as the result of racialization that places groups within a hierarchy as socially privileged or subordinate on the basis of racialized traits. This approach has two virtues, it captures race even if racialization varies from one society to the next. And it explains how race functions in society to uphold hierarchies of power. Cultural constructionists further hold that, even in a world that has achieved racial equality, race would persist as it would be grounded in cultural differences that emerged as a consequence of the history of race and racial struggle.

Anti-realists agree with social constructionists that race is the result of human thought and action. They disagree however that race is a social construct. Rather, racial anti-realists hold that there is nothing in the world that is picked out by a concept that resembles what we broadly mean by *race*. As such, race is neither biologically nor socially real. The race concept ought to be treated in philosophical terms the same way we treat the witch concept.

# References

Allison, A. C. (2002). The discovery of resistance to malaria of sickle-cell heterozygotes. *Biochemistry and Molecular Biology Education, 30,* 279–287. https://doi.org/10.1002/bmb.2002.494030050108.

Andreasen, R. O. (2005). The meaning of "race": Folk conceptions and the new biology of race. *The Journal of Philosophy, 102*(2), 94–106.

Andreasen, R. O. (2004). The cladistic race concept: A defense. *Biology and Philosophy, 19,* 425–442.

Andreasen, R. O. (2000). Race: Biological reality or social construct? *Philosophy of Science, 67*(S3), S653–S666.

Andreasen, R. O. (1998). A new perspective on the race debate. *The British Journal for the Philosophy of Science, 49*(2), 199–225.

Appiah, K. A. (2007). Does truth matter to identity? In Jorge J. E. Garcia (ed.), *Race or Ethnicity? On Black and Latino Identity*, Cornell University Press, pp. 19–44.

Appiah, K. A. (1996). Race, culture, identity: Misunderstood connections. In K. Anthony Appiah and Amy Gutmann (ed.), *Color Conscious*: *The Political Morality of Race*. Princeton University Press, pp. 30–105.

Atlas, J. (1988). Chicago's grumpy guru. *New York Times Magazine.* www .nytimes.com/1988/01/03/magazine/chicago-s-grumpy-guru.html.

Bever, E. (2013). Popular witch beliefs and magical practices. In Brian P. Levack (ed.), *The Oxford Handbook of Witchcraft in Early Modern Europe and Colonial America.* Oxford University Press, pp. 50–69.

Bhogal, H. (2023). The package deal account of naturalness. In Michael Hicks, Siegfried Jaag, and Christian Loew (eds.), *Humean Laws for Human Agents*, Oxford University Press.

Biddanda, A., Rice, D. P., & Novembre, J. (2020). A variant-centric perspective on geographic patterns of human allele frequency variation. *Elife, 9,* 1–23.

Blum, L. (2010). Racialized groups: The sociohistorical consensus. *The Monist, 93*(2), 298–320.

Blum, Lawrence A. (2002). *I'm Not a Racist, but — The Moral Quandary of Race.* Cornell University Press.

Chen, L., Wolf, A. B., Fu, W., Li, L., & Akey, J. M. (2020). Identifying and interpreting apparent Neanderthal ancestry in African individuals. *Cell, 180* (4), 677–687.

Craft, W. (1860). *Running a Thousand Miles for Freedom*: *The Escape of William and Ellen Craft from Slavery.* LSU Press.

Craver, C. F. (2007). *Explaining the Brain: Mechanisms and the Mosaic unity of Neuroscience*. Oxford University Press.

Craver, C. F., & Darden, L. (2013). *In Search of Mechanisms: Discoveries across the Life Sciences*. University of Chicago Press.

DeWindt, A. R. (1995). Witchcraft and conflicting visions of the ideal village community. *Journal of British Studies*, *34*(4), 427–463.

Dikilitas, O., Schaid, D. J., Kosel, M. L., et al. (2020). Predictive utility of polygenic risk scores for coronary heart disease in three major racial and ethnic groups. *The American Journal of Human Genetics*, *106*(5), 707–716.

Ding, K., de Andrade, M., Manolio, T. A., et al. (2013). Genetic variants that confer resistance to malaria are associated with red blood cell traits in African-Americans: An electronic medical record-based genome-wide association study. *G3: Genes, Genomes, Genetics*, *3*(7), 1061–1068.

Evershed, R. P., Davey Smith, G., Roffet-Salque, M., et al. (2022). Dairying, diseases and the evolution of lactase persistence in Europe. *Nature*, *608* (7922), 336–345.

Eze, E. C. (1997). *Race and the Enlightenment: A Reader*. Oxford: Wiley-Blackwell.

Ferreira, A., Marguti, I., Bechmann, I., et al. (2011). Sickle hemoglobin confers tolerance to Plasmodium infection. *Cell*, *145*(3), 398-409.

Fields, B. J. (1982). Ideology and race in American history. In J. Morgan Kousser and James M. McPherson (eds.), *Region, Race, and Reconstruction: Essays in Honor of C. Vann Woodward*. Oxford University Press, pp. 143–177.

Fields, B. J., & Fields, K. E. (2012). *Racecraft: The Soul of Inequality in American Life*. Verso Books.

Fodor, J. A. (1974). Special sciences or the disunity of the sciences as a working hypothesis. *Synthese*, *28*, 97–115.

Franklin-Hall, L. R. (2015). Natural kinds as categorical bottlenecks. *Philosophical Studies*, *172*, 925–948.

Gao, X., & Starmer, J. (2007). Human population structure detection via multi-locus genotype clustering. *BMC genetics*, *8*, 1–11.

Gibson, J. J. (1979). *The Ecological Approach to Visual Perception*. Psychology Press.

Gibson, E. J., & Walk, R. D. (1960). The visual cliff. *Scientific American*, *202*, 64–71.

Glasgow, J. (2009). *A Theory of Race*. Routledge.

Glasgow, J. M. (2003). On the new biology of race. *The Journal of Philosophy*, *100*(9), 456–474.

Glasgow, J., Haslanger, S., Jeffers, C., & Spencer, Q. (2019). *What Is Race?: Four Philosophical Views*. Oxford University Press.

Goodare, J. (2013). Witchcraft in Scotland. In Brian P. Levack (ed.), *The Oxford Handbook of Witchcraft in Early Modern Europe and Colonial America*. Oxford University Press, pp. 300–317.

Goodman, N. ([1955]/1983). *Fact, Fiction, and Forecast*. Harvard University Press.

Gould, S. J. (1996). *Mismeasure of Man*. W. W. Norton.

Hacking, I. (1999). *The Social Construction of What?* Harvard University Press.

Hardimon, M. O. (2017a). *Rethinking Race*. Harvard University Press.

Hardimon, M. O. (2017b). Minimalist biological race. In Naomi Zack (ed.), *The Oxford Handbook of Philosophy and Race*. Oxford University Press, pp. 150–159.

Hardimon, M. O. (2003). The ordinary concept of race. *The Journal of Philosophy, 100*(9), 437–455.

Haslanger, S. (2016). What is a (social) structural explanation? *Philosophical Studies, 173*, 113–130.

Haslanger, S. (2012). *Resisting reality: Social construction and social critique*. Oxford University Press.

Haslanger, S. (2000). Gender and race: (What) are they? (What) do we want them to be? *Noûs, 34*(1), 31–55.

Hellwege, J. N., Keaton, J. M., Giri, A., et al. (2017). Population stratification in genetic association studies. *Current Protocols in Human Genetics, 95*(1), 1–22.

Hirschfeld, L. A. (1996). *Race in the Making: Cognition, Culture, and the Child's Construction of Human Kinds*. MIT Press.

Hochman, A. (2022). Has social constructionism about race outlived its usefulness? Perspectives from a race skeptic. *Biology & Philosophy, 37*(6), 1–20.

Hochman, A. (2017). Replacing race: Interactive constructionism about racialized groups. *Ergo, 4*(3), 61–92.

Hochman, A. (2013). Against the new racial naturalism. *The Journal of Philosophy, 110*(6), 331–351.

Hou, K., Ding, Y., Xu, Z., et al. (2023). Causal effects on complex traits are similar for common variants across segments of different continental ancestries within admixed individuals. *Nature genetics, 55*(4), 549–558.

Hunt, A. N. (2006). *Haiti's Influence on Antebellum America: Slumbering Volcano in the Caribbean*. LSU Press.

Jeffers, C. (2013). The cultural theory of race: Yet another look at Du Bois's "The Conservation of Races." *Ethics, 123*(3), 403–426.

Kalewold, K. H. (2020). Race and medicine in light of the new mechanistic philosophy of science. *Biology & Philosophy, 35*(4), 1–22.

Kaplan J. M., & Winther, R. G. (2014). Realism, antirealism, and conventionalism about race. *Philosophy of Science, 81*(5), 1039–1052.

Kaufman, J. S., Dolman, L., Rushani, D., & Cooper, R. S. (2015). The contribution of genomic research to explaining racial disparities in cardiovascular disease: A systematic review. *American Journal of Epidemiology, 181*(7), 464–472.

Khalidi, M. A. (2018). Natural kinds as nodes in causal networks. *Synthese, 195*, 1379–1396.

Khalifa, K., & Lauer, R. (2021). Do the social sciences vindicate race's reality? *Philosophers Imprint, 21*(21), 2–17.

Kitcher, P. (2007). Does "race" have a future? *Philosophy and Public Affairs, 35*(4), 293–317.

Kitcher, P. (2001). *Science, Truth, and Democracy.* Oxford University Press.

Kitcher, P. (1999). Race, ethnicity, biology, culture. In Leonard Harris (ed.), *Racism*, Humanity Books, pp. 87–117.

Kitcher, P. (2012). *Preludes to Pragmatism: Toward a Reconstruction of Philosophy.* Oxford University Press.

Kleingeld, P. (2007). Kant's second thoughts on race. *The Philosophical Quarterly, 57*(229), 573–592.

Lewis, D. (1983). New work for a theory of universals. *Australasian Journal of Philosophy, 61*(4), 343–377.

Lewontin, R. C. (1972). The apportionment of human diversity. *Evolutionary Biology, 6*, 381–398.

Long, J. C., Li, J., & Healy, M. E. (2009). Human DNA sequences: More variation and less race. *American Journal of Physical Anthropology, 139*(1), 23–34.

Lu-Adler, H. (2023). *Kant, Race, and Racism: Views from Somewhere.* Oxford University Press.

Malik, K. (1996). *The Meaning of Race: Race, History and Culture in Western Society.* Bloomsbury.

Mallon, R. (2018). Constructing race: Racialization, causal effects, or both? *Philosophical Studies, 175*(5), 1039–1056.

Mallon, R. (2017). Social construction and achieving reference. *Noûs 51*(1), 113–131. https://doi.org/10.1111/nous.12107.

Mallon, R. (2006). "Race": Normative, not metaphysical or semantic. *Ethics, 116*(3), 525–551.

Marks, J. (2007). Long shadow of Linnaeus's human taxonomy. *Nature, 447*(7140), 28–28.

Mills, C. W. (1998). *Blackness Visible: Essays on Philosophy and Race*. Cornell University Press.

Moroz, L. L. (2014). The genealogy of genealogy of neurons. *Communicative & Integrative Biology*, *7*(6), 1–6.

Müller-Wille, S. (2014). Race and history: Comments from an epistemological point of view. *Science, Technology, & Human Values*, *39*(4): 597–606.

Outlaw, L. (1996). *On Race and Philosophy*. Routledge.

Pearlman, S. M., Serber, Z., & Ferrell Jr., J. E. (2011). A mechanism for the evolution of phosphorylation sites, *Cell*, *147*(4), 934–946.

Piel, F. B., Steinberg, M. H., & Rees, D. C. (2017). Sickle cell disease. *New England Journal of Medicine*, *376*(16), 1561–1573.

Piel, F. B., Patil, A. P., Howes, R. E., et al. (2010). Global distribution of the sickle cell gene and geographical confirmation of the malaria hypothesis. *Nature Communications*, *1*(1), 1–7.

Pigliucci, M., & Kaplan, J. (2003). On the concept of biological race and its applicability to humans. *Philosophy of Science*, *70*(5), 1161–1172.

Rao, S., Segar, M. W., Bress, A. P., et al. (2020). Association of genetic West African ancestry, blood pressure response to therapy, and cardiovascular risk among self-reported Black individuals in the Systolic Blood Pressure Reduction Intervention Trial (SPRINT). *JAMA Cardiology*, *6*(4), 388–398.

Rasmussen, M., Guo, X., Wang, Y., et al. (2011). An Aboriginal Australian genome reveals separate human dispersals into Asia. *Science*, *334*(6052), 94–98.

Root, M. (2003). The use of race in medicine as a proxy for genetic diferences. *Philosophy of Science*, *70*(5), 1173–1183.

Rosenberg, N. A. (2011). A population-genetic perspective on the similarities and differences among worldwide human populations. *Human Biology*, *83* (6), 659–684.

Rosenberg, N. A., Mahajan, S., Ramachandran, S., et al. (2005). Clines, clusters, and the effect of study design on the inference of human population structure. *PLoS Genetics*, *1*(6), 0660–0671.

Rosenberg, N. A., Pritchard, J. K., Weber, J. L., et al. (2002). Genetic structure of human populations. *Science*, *298*(5602), 2381–2385.

Ross, L. N. (2023). What is social structural explanation? A causal account. *Noûs*, *58*(1), 163–179. https://doi.org/10.1111/nous.12446.

Sesardic, N. (2010). Race: A social destruction of a biological concept. *Biology & Philosophy*, *25*(2), 143–162.

Sesardic, N. (2000). Philosophy of science that ignores science: Race, IQ and heritability. *Philosophy of Science*, *67*(4), 580–602.

Shelby, T. (2005). *We Who Are Dark: The Philosophical Foundations of Black Solidarity*. Harvard University Press.

Shelby, T. (2016). *Dark Ghettos: Injustice, Dissent, and Reform*. Harvard University Press.

Sider, T. (2013). *Writing the Book of the World*. Oxford University Press.

Singh, K., & Wodak, D. (2024). Does Race Best Explain Racial Discrimination? *Philosopher's Imprint, 23*, 24.

Smith, J. E. (2015). *Nature, Human Nature, and Human Difference: Race in Early Modern Philosophy*. Princeton University Press.

Spencer, Q. N. J. (2018). A racial classification for medical genetics. *Philosophical Studies, 175*, 1013–1037.

Spencer, Q. (2014). A radical solution to the race problem. *Philosophy of Science, 81*(5), 1025–1038.

Spencer, Q. (2012). What "biological racial realism" should mean. *Philosophical Studies, 159*, 181–204.

Strevens, M. (2008). *Depth: An Account of Scientific Explanation*. Harvard University Press.

Sundstrom, R. (2002). Race as a human kind. *Philosophy and Social Criticism, 28*(1), 91–115.

Tam, V., Patel, N., Turcotte, M., et al. (2019). Benefits and limitations of genome-wide association studies. *Nature Reviews Genetics, 20*(8), 467–484.

Taylor, P. (2011). Rehabilitating a biological notion of race? A response to Sesardic. *Biology & Philosophy, 26*(3), 469–473.

Telles, E., & Paschel, T. (2014). Who is black, white, or mixed race? How skin color, status, and nation shape racial classification in Latin America. *American Journal of Sociology, 120*(3), 864–907.

UNESCO. (1950). Statement on Race. *UNESCO Digital Library*. https://unesdoc.unesco.org/ark:/48223/pf0000128291.

Varagur, K. (2023). Love in the time of sickle-cell disease. *Harper's Magazine*. https://harpers.org/archive/2023/08/love-in-the-time-of-sickle-cell-disease/.

Weslake, B. (2010). Explanatory depth. *Philosophy of Science, 77*(2), 273–294.

Wiley, R. (1996). *Dark Witness: When Black People Should Be Sacrificed (Again)*. One World/Ballantine.

Williams, T. N., & Weatherall, D. J. (2012). World distribution, population genetics, and health burden of the hemoglobinopathies. *Cold Spring Harbor Perspectives in Medicine, 2*(9), 1–14.

Winsberg, E. (2022). Putting races on the ontological map: A close look at Spencer's "new biologism" of race. *Biology & Philosophy, 37*(6), 1–25.

Wodak, D. (2022). Of witches and white folks. *Philosophy and Phenomenological Research, 104*(3), 587–605.

Woodward, J. (2010). Causation in biology: Stability, specificity, and the choice of levels of explanation. *Biology & Philosophy, 25,* 287–318.

Yudell, M., Roberts, D., DeSalle, R., & Tishkoff, S. (2016). Taking race out of human genetics. *Science, 351*(6273), 564–565.

Zack, N. (2018). *Philosophy of Race: An Introduction.* Palgrave Macmillan.

Zack, N. (2014). *Philosophy of Science and Race.* Routledge.

Zack, N. (1993). *Race and Mixed Race.* Temple University Press.

# Cambridge Elements

# Metaphysics

## Tuomas E. Tahko

*University of Bristol*

Tuomas E. Tahko is Professor of Metaphysics of Science at the University of Bristol, UK. Tahko specializes in contemporary analytic metaphysics, with an emphasis on methodological and epistemic issues: 'meta-metaphysics'. He also works at the interface of metaphysics and philosophy of science: 'metaphysics of science'. Tahko is the author of *Unity of Science* (Cambridge University Press, 2021, *Elements in Philosophy of Science*), *An Introduction to Metametaphysics* (Cambridge University Press, 2015) and editor of *Contemporary Aristotelian Metaphysics* (Cambridge University Press, 2012).

### About the Series

This highly accessible series of Elements provides brief but comprehensive introductions to the most central topics in metaphysics. Many of the Elements also go into considerable depth, so the series will appeal to both students and academics. Some Elements bridge the gaps between metaphysics, philosophy of science, and epistemology.

# Cambridge Elements ☰

# Metaphysics

## Elements in the Series

*Dispositions and Powers*
Toby Friend and Samuel Kimpton-Nye

*Modality*
Sònia Roca Royes

*Indeterminacy in the World*
Alessandro Torza

*Parts and Wholes: Spatial to Modal*
Meg Wallace

*Formal Ontology*
Jani Hakkarainen and Markku Keinänen

*Chemistry's Metaphysics*
Vanessa A. Seifert

*Ontological Categories: A Methodological Guide*
Katarina Perovic

*Abstract Objects*
David Liggins

*Grounding, Fundamentality and Ultimate Explanations*
Ricki Bliss

*Metaphysics and the Sciences*
Matteo Morganti

*Teleology*
Matthew Tugby

*Metaphysics of Race*
Kal H. Kalewold

A full series listing is available at: www.cambridge.org/EMPH